The Contents of Visual Experience

PHILOSOPHY OF MIND SERIES

Series Editor: David J. Chalmers, *Australian National University*

THE CONSCIOUS BRAIN
   Jesse Prinz

SIMULATING MINDS
The Philosophy, Psychology, and Neuroscience of Mindreading
   Alvin I. Goldman

SUPERSIZING THE MIND
Embodiment, Action, and Cognitive Extension
   Andy Clark

PERCEPTION, HALLUCINATION, AND ILLUSION
   William Fish

PHENOMENAL CONCEPTS AND PHENOMENAL
KNOWLEDGE
New Essays on Consciousness and Physicalism
   Torin Alter and Sven Walter

PHENOMENAL INTENTIONALITY
   George Graham, John Tienson and Terry Horgan

THE CHARACTER OF CONSCIOUSNESS
   David J. Chalmers

THE SENSES
Classic and Contemporary Philosophical Perspectives
   Fiona Macpherson

ATTENTION IS COGNITIVE UNISON
An Essay in Philosophical Psychology
   Christopher Mole

THE CONTENTS OF VISUAL EXPERIENCE
   Susanna Siegel

The Contents of
Visual Experience

Susanna Siegel

OXFORD
UNIVERSITY PRESS

OXFORD
UNIVERSITY PRESS

Oxford University Press publishes works that further
Oxford University's objective of excellence
in research, scholarship, and education.

Oxford   New York
Auckland   Cape Town   Dar es Salaam   Hong Kong   Karachi
Kuala Lumpur   Madrid   Melbourne   Mexico City   Nairobi
New Delhi   Shanghai   Taipei   Toronto

With offices in
Argentina   Austria   Brazil   Chile   Czech Republic   France   Greece
Guatemala   Hungary   Italy   Japan   Poland   Portugal   Singapore
South Korea   Switzerland   Thailand   Turkey   Ukraine   Vietnam

Copyright © 2010 by Oxford University Press, Inc.

Published by Oxford University Press
198 Madison Avenue, New York, New York 10016
www.oup.com

First issued as an Oxford University Press paperback, 2012.

Oxford is a registered trademark of Oxford University Press

Siegel, Susanna.
      The contents of visual experience / by Susanna Siegel.
          p. cm. – (Philosophy of mind series)
        ISBN 978-0-19-530529-6 (hardcover); 978-0-19-993124-8 (paperback)
      1. Vision. 2. Experience. 3. Philosophy of mind. I. Title.
B105.V54S53   2010
121'.35–dc22   2010000650

Printed in the United States of America
on acid-free paper

For my friends

Acknowledgments

MUCH OF THE MATERIAL IN THIS BOOK GREW AND MORPHED DURING countless discussions in colloquia, conferences, reading groups and seminars. I'm grateful for those chances to think out loud in the company of so many people held captive by the norms of politeness. I consider myself especially lucky to have received comments and advice from Tim Bayne, Ned Block, Bill Brewer, Alex Byrne, Liz Camp, John Campbell, Jonathan Cohen, Andy Egan, Justin Fisher, Tamar Gendler, John Hawthorne, Benj Hellie, Christopher Hill, Sean Kelly, Amy Kind, Jeff King, Heather Logue, Fiona Macpherson, John Morrison, Ram Neta, Bernhard Nickel, Casey O'Callaghan, Adam Pautz, Christopher Peacocke, Geoffrey Sayre-McCord, Joshua Schechter, Charles Siewert, Nico Silins, David Woodruff Smith, Maja Spener, Jason Stanley, Daniel Stoljar, Scott Sturgeon, Amie Thomasson, Joseph Tolliver, Charles Travis, Jonathan Vogel, and Jessica Wilson. I've learned much from the luminous writings of Mark Johnston, M. G. F. Martin and A. D. Smith. I've also been helped immensely by my friendships with Alex Byrne, Bernhard Nickel, Scott Sturgeon and Maja Spener. Alex co-taught a graduate seminar with me on some of the material in part I, read multiple drafts of most of the chapters, and over the years has pulled me out of numerous bogs. Bernhard, Scott and Maja discussed every topic in the book with me at length, generating countless insights, innovations, jokes, meals and cocktails along the way.

In 2002 I presented an early draft of a paper defending the Rich Content View at the National Endowment for the Humanities seminar on consciousness and intentionality. The institute as a whole brought the depth of many of the issues surrounding that view into focus. I'm grateful to the members of the institute and to its co-director, David Chalmers, for helping to shape the broader context in which I began writing this book. David's manner creates philosophical spaces that are friendly, open, and rigorous—an enlivening antidote to individualistic settings that can crush the spirit and close the mind. He has helped build vibrant communities of philosophers in diverse ways, through conferences, online projects, his commitment to helping younger philosophers, and his sheer philosophical life-force. In different ways these undertakings have helped bring this project to life.

The material in chapters 1, 2, and 6 and 8 is entirely new, and though parts of chapters 3, 4, 5, and 7 are based on previously published papers, this material has been revised and often rewritten from the ground up. Chapter 2 appears simultaneously in *Perceiving the World*, edited by Bence Nanay (Oxford University Press, 2010).

Thanks are also due to Greta Platt and Jigmae for their warm hospitality. Most of this book was written in their Somerville café.

Table of Contents

The Contents of Visual Experience

Introduction

Suppose you are looking out at the street. you see people interacting with things and with each other. They walk past trees, ride bicycles, and get into cars. Seeing such scenes does not usually demand much effort of interpretation. You can just see that someone is talking to the person next to her, getting into a car, or riding a bicycle.

Suddenly you notice one of the people on the street. It's John Malkovich! He's carrying a little dog in his arms. What part of this exciting occurrence belongs to your perception, and which to subsequent judgment? Is it already part of your visual experience that John Malkovich is walking by, carrying a dog? Or do you just visually experience an array of colored shapes bouncing slightly at regular intervals, and subsequently judge that it is John Malkovich carrying a dog? More generally, we can ask: Do you just visually experience arrays of colored shapes, variously illuminated, and sometimes moving? Or does visual experience involve more-complex features, such as personal identity, causation, and kinds of objects, such as bicycles, keys, and cars?

These questions are about conscious experience. Visual experience is a kind of conscious mental state. A visual experience is one of the states (among many others) that you are in when you see things. There is "something it is like" to have a visual experience, and what it's like varies with what you see, what you pay attention to, and your perceptual idiosyncracies, such as astigmatism, colorblindness, whether your cornea is scratched, whether you are wearing corrective lenses, and so on. All of these factors contribute to the specific conscious or phenomenal character of a visual experience, or equivalently, to what it is like to have it. We can call this *visual phenomenal character*, or *visual phenomenology*, for short.

This book is an exploration of how things may look to us in our visual experiences of them. I pursue this question by asking which properties are represented in visual experience. This way of framing the issue relies on the Content View, a general thesis that experiences have contents. I will argue for a specific version of the Content View: the Rich Content View, according to which the contents of visual experience are richly complex, and so are not limited to color, shape, and other properties standardly taken to be represented in visual experience.

THE CONTENT VIEW

What does it mean to say that properties are represented in visual experience? The notion of representation is tied to the idea that experiences have contents, where contents are a kind of condition under which experiences are accurate, similar in many ways to the truth-conditions of beliefs. I call this thesis the Content View. The Content View serves as a framework within which the Rich Content View can be assessed. In what follows it plays an important instrumental role. But the Content View is also of interest in its own right, and the first two chapters of this book are devoted to its clarification and defense.

Beliefs are paradigms of mental states that can be true or false. In early modern philosophy, perception is often construed as a special kind of input to belief that differs from belief in fundamental ways. Think of Hume's distinction between ideas and impressions. The idea that experiences, like beliefs, could be accurate or inaccurate has come to play a central role in contemporary discussions. On the one hand, some philosophers (relatively few in number) have attacked the idea that experiences can be understood as any kind of representation at all. On the other hand, in debates about phenomena as diverse as perceptual constancies, inverted spectra, the existence of qualia, and linguistic reference, many philosophers have regarded the idea that experiences can be accurate or inaccurate as a background assumption that is too obvious (or at least, too reasonable) to require much explanation.[1] Is it really one and the same idea that some take as obvious and that others take as dead wrong?

To work through this question, the Content View needs to be examined more closely. In part I, I argue that the Content View is a substantive thesis that requires defense, but that its defense is much more widely acceptable than is often supposed.

The Content View is often thought to belong to an outlook in which visual experiences form a single kind of mental state encompassing hallucinations along with perceptions, and that when such states are phenomenally alike, they have exactly the same contents.[2] I'll call this cluster of theses the *internalist outlook*. Why is the Content View associated with the internalist outlook? The association comes from construing contents using intentional objects as a model. Suppose you are looking for Pete from Pluto, or hallucinating a pink cat. Whether or not Pete or pink cats exist, it is natural for you to *say* "I see a pink cat" or "I'm looking for Pete." Assigning Pete or a pink cat the status of an intentional object seems to make this way of talking coherent. You're looking for Pete, not Martian Mary. You're hallucinating a pink cat, not a green lion. To proponents of the internalist outlook, just as it can

---

1. For instance, the view is taken for granted in Evans (1982), Peacocke (1992), and in contemporary discussions of color experience, such as Block (1990) and Byrne and Hilbert (1997). It is attacked by Martin (2002), Campbell (2002), Brewer (2006), Travis (2005), and Robinson (1994). Robinson's criticisms come from a different direction and focus on Anscombe's version (1965) of the idea that experiences have contents.

2. This outlook is a locus of attack by Martin (2002), Campbell (2002), Brewer (2006), and Travis (2005).

be natural to say "I see a pink cat" when there are no pink cats, so too it is natural to think of perceptions and hallucinations as sharing exactly the same contents if they are phenomenally the same. To this extent, these proponents take contents to play many of the same basic theoretical roles as intentional objects.[3]

Chapter 2 makes the case that the Content View can be divorced from the internalist outlook and its construal of contents. Whether that outlook should be rejected is a separate question of interest in its own right. But one could see the book as urging that this outlook—whether true or false—is in some ways less important to the philosophy of perception than many suppose. We need not orient our thinking around it as a fault line in order to make philosophical progress. Without either accepting or rejecting the internalist outlook, we can discover that experiences have contents, and we can discover which contents those are.

THE RICH CONTENT VIEW

Standardly, color, shape, illumination, motion, and their co-instantiation in objects are taken to be represented in visual experience. In this book I argue that much of what we understand about the things we see is part of visual phenomenology itself. Visual phenomenology can be an input to recognition and categorization,

3. Not all proponents of the internalist outlook go as far as identifying contents with intentional objects. Some puzzling questions arise once this identification is made. In what relations, if any, can we stand in to nonexistent intentional objects such as Pete from Pluto? If you and I both want to meet Pete, do our desires have the same intentional object, or different ones? If you come to believe that Pete is from Mars instead of Pluto, does the intentional object of your desire to meet him change? The difficulty of answering these questions may motivate internalists to avoid intentional objects, even if they want their notion of content to play the same theoretical roles that intentional objects are invoked to play.

but it is not itself always devoid of information (and misinformation) about which categories and kinds things belong to and what relations of causal dependence they stand in. I argue that some visual experiences represent properties other than the ones standardly taken to be so represented. Although these other properties do not form a natural class, it will be useful to have a label for them. Because they include kind properties (though they're not limited to kind properties), I'm going to call them *K-properties*. I call the thesis that K-properties are represented in perception the Rich Content View[4]:

> **Rich Content View**: In some visual experiences, some properties other than spatial properties, color, shape, motion, and illumination are represented.

For instance, if your experience represents that it's John Malkovich walking by, or that he is carrying something, or that it's a dog, then the Rich Content View is true.

WHY DOES IT MATTER?

The Rich Content View bears on some traditional philosophical questions and is also closely connected to several areas of psychological research. The traditional philosophical problems it bears on include the problem of intentionality, skepticism about the external world, the scope of the perceptual interface, and the rational role of experiences vis à vis beliefs and judgment.

The problem of intentionality is sometimes posed by asking what makes it the case that contentful states have the contents they do. This question is extremely difficult to answer. Despite a great amount of philosophical toil, we are still a long way from understanding what makes mental states have the contents they

---

4. In Siegel (2006) the same thesis is called *Thesis K*.

do, either for the case of visual experience or for any other mental states. Given the difficulties of constructing a theory of intentionality, it may be useful to concentrate on finding constraints on such theories. A verdict on the Rich Content View places a constraint on accounts of theories of intentionality for visual experience. If visual experience can represent that there are peaches on the table, then whatever makes it the case that a visual experience has the content it does had better not disallow that visual experiences represent the properties of being a peach or a table.

The Rich Content View can also inform debates surrounding skepticism about the external world. There may be general skeptical worries that get going only if the contents of visual experience turn out to be informationally impoverished in a way that is incompatible with the Rich Content View. For example, suppose that veridical experiences could provide information only about the colors and facing surfaces of objects, and not about which facing surfaces belong to the same object, or whether or not they continue out of view. Could such visual experiences play the justificatory role claimed for them by a correct theory of justification? Someone might reasonably doubt that they could. Settling which contents visual experiences have will determine whether such a challenge is worth attempting to formulate.

The Rich Content View also bears on the scope of possible perceptual contact with reality. If perception is such an interface, then it is a channel through which we can end up with information about our environment. What does conscious experience contribute to the interface? If the Rich Content View is false, then, at best, visual experience could put us in contact with colors, shapes, motion, and luminance properties. Any representations of properties other than these would not have the same status (or even apparent status) as inputs from the environment. If the Rich Content View is true, then in whatever way we can be in contact with a thing's shape and color, we can likewise be in contact with other properties of the things we see, such as a thing's being a hand (part of an animate body), its weighing down a hammock (a causal property), or its walking down the street carrying a dog. If a property can figure only in representations that are downstream of conscious experience, then we cannot be in perceptual contact with those properties. Now, not every visual experience is a case of perceptual contact with reality. There are hallucinations, illusions, and other cases in which perceptual contact fails, and these failures won't be ignored in the chapters that follow. But if we want to understand what kinds of inputs conscious perception can provide, we should focus on whether the Rich Content View is true.

Finally, the Rich Content View bears on the role of experiences in the formation of reasonable beliefs and judgments. We can distinguish between two roles in this domain, which we can call *doxastic* and *propositional*. The doxastic role is the role of experience in the actual process that the subject undergoes (or that the subject's subpersonal mechanisms undergo) in forming beliefs or judgments. Presumably, that process is causal, and when we ask what doxastic role experience plays, we are asking how experience figures in that causal process and how it contributes to the status of the resulting doxastic states as reasonable (or unreasonable). In contrast, when we ask what propositional role an experience plays, we are asking which beliefs or judgments the experience makes it reasonable to form—whether or not the subject actually forms those beliefs.

It could turn out that conscious visual experience has no doxastic role to play. Perhaps if you could excise conscious visual experience from the picture while leaving all other aspects of visual processing intact, subjects would hold the same beliefs and form the same judgments, and those beliefs and judgments would have the same epistemic status. It is a substantive thesis that conscious experience is irrelevant to doxastic justification in this way. If it is irrelevant, then whether the Rich Content View is true wouldn't much matter at all to doxastic justification. But if conscious experience could not be excised without affecting doxastic justification, then whether or not the Rich Content View is true may help determine which beliefs and judgments are doxastically justified.

When it comes to propositional justification, the importance of the Rich Content View seems less of a hostage to philosophical fortune. Whatever role experience may have in doxastic justification, since we can sensibly ask what reasons specific visual experiences offer for beliefs and judgments, experiences can provide propositional justification for beliefs or judgments. And which propositions experiences provide evidential support for depends, in turn, on whether the Rich Content View is true.

The Rich Content View is also related to the idea that visual experience can be theory-laden, or influenced by other mental states through cognitive penetration. This kind of influence complicates the epistemic role of experience. If experience can be influenced by beliefs to begin with, then what happens to its status as a tribunal that can be used to test beliefs against the world?[5] One kind of argument for the Rich Content View relies on the idea that non-perceptual mental states can influence the contents of visual experience. According to this kind of argument, a K-property such as the property of being a pine tree can come to be represented in visual experience partly in virtue of your disposition to recognize pine trees when you see them. If so, then your visual experience would be cognitively penetrated by the mental states associated with your recognitional disposition. Now, the Rich Content View itself does not entail that visual experiences can be cognitively penetrated.[6] But one kind of argument for the Rich Content View—a kind I myself give in chapter 4—in effect brings phenomenological considerations to bear on a controversy

5. This question has most often been discussed in connection with the role of observation in science. Classic papers include Fodor (1984, 1988), Churchland (1988), and Pylyshyn (1999). More recent work includes Stokes (forthcoming), Macpherson (2012), Raftopoulos (2009), and Siegel (2011).

6. And conversely, the Rich Content View is not entailed by the thesis that visual experiences are cognitively penetrable. In principle, the influence of non-perceptual states on the contents of visual experience might be limited to non-K properties.

in psychology about the extent to which visual experience is insulated from other expectations, recognitional dispositions, and other mental states.[7]

Aside from its bearing on philosophical issues, the Rich Content View is relevant to several other areas of research in psychology and neuroscience.

First, the scientific study of consciousness looks to find neural correlates of consciousness. Where should we look for neural correlates of conscious visual experience? Whether the Rich Content View is true will influence what we will count as a neural correlate of visual experience. If the view is false, then we might expect to find these neural correlates in brain areas devoted to "early" visual processing, such as visual areas V1 and V5. If the view is true, then we should expect neural correlates to involve "later" areas, such as the fusiform face area (FFA) and the inferotemporal cortex (IT).

7. A range of empirical studies in social psychology, color vision, object categorization, and gaze fixation suggest that visual experiences are sometimes heavily influenced by antecedent knowledge, beliefs, desires, goals, or moods. Among studies in social psychology, Payne (2001) presents evidence that people exposed to black faces were more likely to misidentify a tool as a gun under time pressure, and Eberhardt et al. (2004) found that white subjects primed with images of black faces more readily detect guns in fuzzy images, compared with subjects primed with white faces. Similar priming results can be found with object categorization generally (Kverga et al. 2009). In the domain of color vision, Hansen et al. (2006) argue that beliefs about what color bananas are influence the color things appear to you to be when you believe they are bananas (an achromatic banana will look yellowish). Broackes (2010) discusses a case in which expectations about what color a thing should be influences the color experience of colorblind subjects, and D. T. Levin and M. R. Banaji (2006) give evidence that categorizing a racially ambiguous face as "black" or "white" influences how light subjects perceive it to be. For discussions of the influence of mood on perception, see Barrett et al. (2009) and Barrick et al. (2002). On gaze fixation, see Triesch et al. (2003).

Second, the Rich Content View bears on debates in psychiatry about the nature of some delusions that involve perceptual experience. For example, in Capgras syndrome, patients seem to believe that people close to them have been replaced by impostors. To assess and ultimately treat this cognitive disorder, it is useful to know whether the delusion is a normal response to an unusual experience, an unusual response to an unusual experience, or an unusual response to a normal experience. Is the property of being an impostor one that can be represented in visual experience? More generally, some symptoms of schizophrenia involve forming (and sticking to) bizarre beliefs about one's environment. We can ask what role perceptual experiences play in those beliefs. If philosophy finds independent support for the Rich Content View, it can help us decide whether such disorders involve normal responses to unusual experiences, or whether they reside entirely in unusual responses to normal experiences.[8]

Third, whether the Rich Content View is true makes a difference as to how best to understand the structure of associative agnosia. Associative agnosics cannot identify common objects that they see, or describe what they are used for, though they can often identify them and their utility by touch. Early observers of patients with this condition described it as follows:

> For the first three weeks in the hospital the patient could not identify common objects presented visually and did not know what was on his plate until he tasted it. He identified objects immediately on touching them. When shown a stethoscope, he described it as "a long cord with a round thing at the end," and asked if it could be a watch. He identified a can opener as "could be a key." Asked to name a cigarette lighter, he said, "I don't know," but named it after the examiner lit it. He said he was "not sure" when shown a toothbrush. Asked to identify a comb, he said, "I don't know." When shown a large matchbook,

8. For discussion of possible explanations in this area, see Davies and Coltheart (2000).

he said, "It could be a container for keys." He correctly identified glasses. For a pipe, he said, "Some type of utensil, I'm not
sure." Shown a key, he said, "I don't know what that is; perhaps
a file or a tool of some sort." He was never able to describe or
demonstrate the use of an object if he could not name it. If he
misnamed an object, his demonstration of its use would correspond to the mistaken identification. . . . Remarkably, he could
make excellent copies of line drawings and still fail to name the
subject. . . . He easily matched drawings of objects that he could
not identify, and had no difficulty in discriminating between
complex non-representational patterns differing from each
other only subtly. He occasionally failed in discriminating
because he included imperfections in the paper or in the printer's
ink. He could never group drawings by class unless he could
first name the subject.[9] (Rubens & Benson 1971: 308–9)

If the Rich Content View is false, then the contents of associative
agnosics' visual experiences may be no more impoverished than
those of the rest of us, and the deficit in associative agnosia may
be purely a matter of responses to conscious experience. In contrast, if the Rich Content View is true, then part of the deficit in
associative agnosia may be that the contents of visual experience
are abnormally impoverished.

HOW CAN WE DECIDE WHETHER THE RICH CONTENT VIEW IS TRUE?

It is a broadly empirical question whether the Rich Content View
is true. We can't find the answer by reasoning from first principles
alone. How can the question be answered? To discover whether
the Rich Content View is true, we need a way to investigate the
contents of visual consciousness. Given the nature of conscious

9. For further discussion of the relationship between agnosia and the
Rich Content View, see Bayne (2009).

states, introspection is a natural starting point for investigating whether the Rich Content View is true. Imagine how strange it would be if none of us had the slightest idea what color or shape things looked to us to be. We are not completely blind to what we experience. How could we be, and still have conscious experiences at all? By their nature, conscious experiences have a felt character. This suggests that introspection should have some role in telling us about their nature.

When it comes to the Rich Content View, however, introspection takes us only so far. No matter how much you introspect, it isn't obvious one way or another whether according to your visual experience, it is Malkovich or someone with a specific appearance. Or at least, there is little agreement across subjects about which hypothesis is obvious upon introspective reflection. Apparently, the Rich Content View can't be verified or disconfirmed by introspection alone. This leaves us with a methodological problem. We need a method that respects the felt character of conscious visual experience but yet does not rely on introspection to answer a question that it apparently has no answer to.

In this book, I explicate, defend, and employ such a method: the method of phenomenal contrast. This method can be used to test hypotheses about the nature and contents of visual experiences. I introduce the method in part I (chapter 3). In part II (chapters 4–5) I argue that when the method is applied to the Rich Content View, it yields the result that certain K-properties—kind properties and a wide variety of causal properties—are represented in visual experience, and so the Rich Content View is true. Part III turns to the role of objects in experience. Chapter 6 asks whether, when you see John Malkovich, the contents of your experience could be the same as the contents of the experience you have when you see a Malkovich impostor. The answer offered is: yes and no. When you see John Malkovich, your experience has two sets of contents. One set, the nonsingular contents, could in principle be shared by an experience of seeing a Malkovich impostor (or by a hallucination), while the other set, the singular contents, could not.

Another question about objects concerns the difference between perceptions of ordinary objects, such as cups, cars, and keys, and experiences traditionally classified as visual sensations, such as "seeing stars" from being hit on the head, or having phosphenes. Chapter 7 focuses on the phenomenological differences between these two kinds of visual experiences and argues that there are systematic differences as to which properties each kind of visual experience represents. A special pair of K-properties is represented in standard visual–perceptual experiences but is missing from visual sensations. This pair of K-properties is a pair of perceptual relations between the perceiver and the ordinary objects she perceives.

By the end of the book, three main conclusions about experience are defended. First, experiences have contents. Second, they represent a variety of K-properties, and we can confirm the Rich Content View using the method of phenomenal contrast. Third, they can have both singular and nonsingular contents. All three of these conclusions are defended while bypassing many fascinating but often somewhat tangled debates concerning the underlying nature of phenomenal states. Taken together, they lead to a single upshot: the method of phenomenal contrast, the Content View, and the Rich Content View all have broad application and can be used widely in the analysis of perception.

PART I

CONTENTS

Chapter I

Experiences

IMAGINE THAT YOU ARE WATERSKIING. YOU FEEL THE BOAT PULL you along, adjust your weight to keep your balance, hear the motor rumbling through the water, see your friend Franco steering. The first few times you waterski you are preoccupied about falling. But once you get the hang of it, you can relax and pay attention to things like the pattern of clouds in the sky.

When you waterski you are in a conscious state with many facets. We can call your overall conscious state during the stretch of time that you are waterskiing your *overall experience*. Your overall experience includes seeing the boat and its surroundings, hearing its motor, feeling preoccupied, keeping your balance, and so on. Some of these aspects are deeply coordinated with one another, such as seeing and feeling the boat starting to veer to the right. Here you have two different sensory links to the same event. Other aspects of your experiences are not coordinated in this way. When you see a cloud and notice that it looks like a crocodile, or when you see Franco waving at you from the boat, you don't have any other sensory link to the cloud or to Franco.

From the many facets of waterskiing, we can zoom in on the visual ones. These include:

- seeing Franco, seeing the boat's color, seeing that your boat is behind a bigger boat,
- seeing the boat slow down and turn while you feel yourself slow down and turn, and
- seeing a cloud in the sky as a crocodile.

Consider the state of seeing Franco. What it's like to see Franco is different on different occasions. Sometimes he's driving the boat; other times he's curled up in a chair. When he's at the steering wheel with his head turned toward you, he looks different than he does when he's in pajamas falling asleep in his chair. But there is always something that it is like to see Franco, even though what it's like is not the same every time.

These observations about Franco illustrate a conceptual distinction. Let's say that *phenomenal states* are individuated by what it is like to be in them. In order to be in the same phenomenal state on two different occasions, what it's like to be in that state has to be the same both times. The state of seeing Franco is not identical to a phenomenal state, because there's no unique phenomenal state for it to be identical to. But it is closely related to phenomenal states, because whenever you see Franco, you're in a phenomenal state. Let's say that a state is *phenomenally conscious* when necessarily, in order to be in it, you have to be in a phenomenal state. It is then trivially true that phenomenal states are phenomenally conscious—since every time you're in a phenomenal state, you're in a phenomenal state.[1]

Once we've distinguished between phenomenal and phenomenally conscious states, we can zoom in on specifically visual aspects of the overall experience of waterskiing in two ways. First, we can consider the overall phenomenal state you're in when you're waterskiing, and zoom in on the visual phenomenal state. By doing this, we get to visual experiences that I'll say belong to the narrow class of visual experiences. Visual experiences in the narrow class are phenomenal states. Second, we can consider the overall experience as a collection of phenomenally conscious states and then ignore the non-visual ones. By doing this, we get to visual experiences that I'll say belong to the broad class. The broad class may include a range of ontologically distinct elements,

1. For a similar distinction, see Bayne and Chalmers (2003, sect. 3).

such as episodes, actions, and states of various sorts.[2] For us its most important elements will be states of seeing. Let us examine one kind of state of seeing more closely: states of "seeing-as," such as the state of seeing the cloud as a crocodile.

What is it to see a cloud as a crocodile? On a construal of such states associated loosely with Thomas Reid, if you see a cloud as a crocodile, then you have a "raw feel" that affects you only sensorily (Reid would call it a sensation), together with a judgment, or something akin to a judgment, representing the cloud as a crocodile. Whatever kind of representation is involved in seeing a cloud as a crocodile is confined to one factor, and whatever phenomenal character is involved is confined to a separate factor. This view of seeing-as is inspired by Reid because Reid took all perceptions, not just states of seeing-as, to consist of two components akin to the ones just described.[3]

The Reid-inspired view of seeing-as states is an instance of the more general idea that when you see a cloud as a crocodile, the phenomenal features of your state are confined to just one factor, a different factor represents crocodile-hood, and either factor could exist in the absence of the other. The phenomenal factor need not be a Reidian sensation—it could represent other properties besides crocodile-hood. What's important in this two-factor view is that if you went from seeing the cloud as a hotdog to instead seeing it as a crocodile, your visual phenomenal state would stay the same. Even if, contra Reid, perception does not always have this structure, perhaps some perceptual states are structured this way. For instance, if the person you're talking to looks a bit like a monkey, perhaps in some sense you see her differently when you see her as a monkey, even though your visual

---

2. For discussions probing the ontological status of experiences in the broad sense, see Hinton (1967), Byrne (2009), Johnston (2006), and Hellie (ms).

3. For discussion, see Nichols (2007).

phenomenal state stays the same. Construed broadly, your visual experience changes when you start to see her as a monkey, whereas construed narrowly, your visual experience stays the same.

Neither the Content View nor the Rich Content View is very interesting when applied to visual experiences of seeing-as that are structured by two factors as described above. The Content View would be true of those states, thanks to their representational factor, and the Rich Content View would be true if that factor ever represents K-properties. It is no surprise that judgments have contents, or that they can represent K-properties. For this reason, the Content View and the Rich Content View are theses about visual experiences in the narrow sense: visual phenomenal states. The Content View is the thesis that all visual phenomenal states have contents. The Rich Content View is the thesis that some visual phenomenal states represent K-properties.

1.1 STATES OF SEEING AND PHENOMENAL STATES

Since the Content View and the Rich Content View are about phenomenal states, to get a feel for the scope of these theses, we need to consider the extent of the class of phenomenal states. I've argued that seeing Franco is not a phenomenal state. But what about the more specific state of seeing Franco when he looks sad to you? Are any states of seeing phenomenal states?

At least four assumptions suggest that no states of seeing are phenomenal states. The first two of these assumptions have some intuitive force, whereas the status of the last two is less clear.

First, consider the state of seeing Franco when he looks sad to you. Now suppose you see Franco's twin. Could your state of seeing Franco's twin be phenomenally the same as the state of seeing Franco? If so, then the state of seeing Franco when he looks sad is not a phenomenal state.

Second, suppose you hallucinate someone looking sad. Could your hallucination be phenomenally the same as the state of seeing Franco when he looks sad to you? If so, then the state of seeing Franco when he looks sad is not a phenomenal state.

Third, consider the state of seeing a cloud as a crocodile. If you saw the same cloud as a hotdog instead, could your experience be phenomenally the same? If so, then states of seeing-as are not phenomenal states (as per the two-factor theories of seeing-as).

Fourth, suppose you see Franco on two different occasions. To simplify greatly, suppose that each time he looks to have only two properties: being sad, and being red in the face. Could what it's like to see Franco each time differ, even though the properties he looks to have each time are the same? If so, then the state of seeing an object having a property is not a phenomenal state.

All four of these assumptions are controversial. Some forms of Naïve Realism deny the first two assumptions, and hold that any state of seeing an object or having a property F (or a cluster of properties) is a phenomenal state. And though the two-factor theories of seeing-as endorse the third assumption, other theories of seeing-as would deny it. If any states of seeing are phenomenal states, they fall within the scope of the Content View and the Rich Content View.

I will argue in chapter 6 that no states of seeing are phenomenal states. One might worry that this limits the scope of the Content View and the Rich Content View in such a way that these theses are not true of states of seeing. But the main arguments for each thesis can be straightforwardly extended to many states of seeing, regardless of whether those states of seeing are phenomenal states. So even though eventually I'll argue that we should deny that states of seeing are phenomenal states, this will not put all states of seeing off-limits to the Content View or to the Rich Content View.

1.2 VISUAL PERCEPTUAL EXPERIENCES

In most visual experiences, one sees ordinary objects, such as cups, keys, and bicycles. When we look beyond paradigmatic visual experiences, we find visual experiences that are harder to classify. Think of the visual experience you have when you face a light source with your eyes closed (pink glow), or the visual experience you have when you simply close your eyes (brain gray) or when you experience phosphenes (glowing color patches that appear when you close your eye and gently press your eyeball). There are also mixed experiences, in which one sees or seems to see ordinary objects or scenes, but which also include stranger visual elements, such as phosphenes or "stars" of the sort that appear if you are hit on the head (these are often depicted in cartoons as flecks that swirl around the head of a dazed character). For instance, if you stand up too quickly before breakfast or after taking in too much caffeine, you might "see stars," but you won't thereby cease to see the room that you are in. Here the "stars" are apparently superimposed on the scene that you see, in much the same way that an afterimage is, and the overall visual experience contains elements that have traditionally been classified as visual sensations, or entoptic phenomena.[4] In this book, experiences such as seeing brain gray when one's eyes are closed in the dark or seeing pink glow when one's eyes are closed facing a light source will be sidelined.

It is not easy to characterize with ontological precision how entoptic phenomena are related to the visual perceptual experiences in which they occur. Are they parts of the perceptual experience? Are they aspects of it? These questions recur with respect to the relationships between visual experiences and overall conscious states, and between visual experiences and experiences in other modalities. Characterizing these relationships is one aspect

4. A. Bennett and R. Rabbetts (2004, chap. 22).

of the problem of the unity of consciousness, and I am not going to try to characterize any of them precisely here.[5]

Just as it is difficult to characterize the relationship between more local and more encompassing experiences, it is not always obvious how overall experiences are divided in the first place. Some divisions seem straightforward. If the boat's motor were just noticeably quieter, or if the air didn't smell quite so fresh, the scenery might nonetheless look the same—or so it seems natural to suppose.[6] But in other cases, we can't fix on a specifically visual part of an experience by focusing on what the visual experience would be like in the absence of experiences in other modalities, because in their absence the visual phenomenal state would differ. Consider a case in which you see and feel the boat veer to the right. Perhaps seeing the boat veer to the right differs phenomenally, depending on whether you are also feeling it veer to the right. Or perhaps the boat looks as if it is pulling your arms away from you, but it wouldn't look this way if you didn't have any sensations of being pulled. Do such visual–kinesthetic experiences have a purely visual phenomenal component, or are they irreducibly multimodal?

These questions can be avoided by focusing on visual experiences in which one does not (and does not even seem to) stand in any other sensory link to exactly the same things. There is reason to focus on such experiences in any case, since the Rich Content View is less interesting when applied to certain multimodal experiences, compared with purely visual experiences. For instance,

5. For discussions of the relation between local phenomenal states and the overall conscious state of a person at a time, see Dainton (2000), Shoemaker (1996), and Bayne and Chalmers (2003). Tye (2003) rejects the assumption that that there are multiple experiences but preserves the idea that some phenomenal states are aspects of one big experience.

6. Dainton (2000) discusses the idea that parts of an overall phenomenal state could not possibly occur except in overall states of the same or similar type. (See the discussion of Strong Impingement in his chapter 8, where he argues that cases of Strong Impingement are rare.)

the idea that an auditory–visual experience represents that a blue
sphere is emitting a noise (emitting is a causal notion), or that a
visual and kinesthetic experience represents that your hand is
pulling open a zipper (another causal notion) is somewhat less
surprising than corresponding theses about what visual experiences represent when we ignore auditory and bodily experiences.
So it will maximize the punch of the Content View and the Rich
Content View if we focus on visual experiences that are not multimodal in either of these ways. When formulating these views, I'll
take the relevant visual experiences to exclude visual phenomenal
states that are parts of multimodal experiences in which exactly
the same objects and properties are perceived visually and
through another sensory modality. The main arguments for the
Content View and the Rich Content View could be expanded to
cover various multimodal experiences, but I will not expand their
defenses here.[7]

Summing up, the Content View and the Rich Content View are
theses about visual phenomenal states. I'll call the visual phenomenal states that the Content View and the Rich Content View
are about *visual perceptual experiences*. These experiences exclude
marginal experiences such as pink glow and brain gray, and may
or may not involve entoptic phenomena. Some visual perceptual
experiences figure in states of seeing, while others are hallucinations in which no such objects are seen, though it seems from a
first-person perspective that they are.

7. An argument for the Rich Content View, when applied to jointly
visual and kinesthetic experience, is given in Siegel (2005), where I argue
that these experiences represent *efficacy*, a kind of first-person causation.

Chapter 2

The Content View

If you want to know whether there is any mustard in the refrigerator, it is a good idea to open the door and look. If you see the mustard, you can end up knowing its whereabouts: it's in the fridge. If instead of looking for the mustard, you pictured the fridge interior in a daydream, and then relied on your daydream to confirm whether or not the fridge contained mustard, you wouldn't end up knowing anything about the mustard or the fridge, but you might nevertheless end up with a true or false belief.

As the mustard example illustrates, it is common to regard perception as a special kind of input to belief that allows us to compare hypotheses with the world so that we may assess whether those hypotheses are true. Even philosophers who were cautious about assigning perception more than a causal role in relation to knowledge regard perception as involving a special sort of input to the mind, different in kind from belief and judgment. Hume distinguished impressions from ideas, while Locke found special inputs in the vicinity of perceptual experience, distinguishing ideas of sensations from ideas of reflection. Both in common practice and in philosophy, perception is regarded as a distinctive kind of mental state that serves as an input to belief, and is distinct from it.

Despite the differences between perception and belief, perception involves states that are importantly similar to beliefs: visual experiences, where these include visual hallucinations of ordinary objects and scenes. This chapter interprets, develops, and defends an important thesis about visual perceptual experiences.

27

THE CONTENT VIEW: All visual perceptual experiences
have contents.

The Content View will serve as a framework within which we
will assess the Rich Content View. This chapter explains what the
Content View says, and argues that its commitments are shared
across a wide range of philosophical theories of perception. I'll
sometimes use *experience* without the modifier *visual perceptual*, as
a shorthand.

The kind of content at issue in the Content View meets two
constraints. Contents are true or false, and the contents of an
experience are conveyed to the subject by her experience.[1] The
sense in which experiences have contents (according to the Content View) thus picks up the strand of ordinary usage that takes
contents to be things conveyed by sources of information (as
when we speak of the contents of a newspaper story). Experience
contents need not individuate experiences. And we can, apparently, ostend experiences by using introspection or by describing
the circumstances in which the experience is had, without first
settling whether experiences have any contents at all, let alone
which contents (if any) they have.

In contemporary discussions, the Content View is widely held
and is even presupposed in many debates about perceptual experience.[2] But some philosophers have objected to it on the basis of
Naïve Realism, claiming that Naïve Realism is the more com-
monsensical view, and in one case finding precedent for it in

1. A third constraint will be introduced shortly: contents are accuracy conditions.
2. The Content View has the status of an undefended presupposition
in Evans (1982) and Peacocke (1992), and in debates about whether phenomenal character supervenes on representational features, such as
having content e.g., Block (1990, 1996), Chalmers (2004), Egan (2006),
Kind (2007), Levine (2003), Pace (2007), Rey (1998), Speaks (2009), Tye
(2003), Wright (2003), Thompson (2009), and others.

Berkeley.[3] Naïve Realism comes in a variety of forms, but the main idea (to be qualified later) is that some phenomenal states are identical with certain states of seeing, and so involve relations to objects in the environment. One might think that this view is incompatible with the Content View, perhaps on the grounds that if experiences involve relations to the objects in an environment, they do not involve relations to contents. I will argue that standard versions of Naïve Realism are compatible with the Content View. To oppose the Content View, Naïve Realism would have to take a radical form that leaves out reference to properties. The resulting versions of Naïve Realism, I'll argue, are implausible. More generally, I'll argue that once the role of properties in phenomenal character is acknowledged, the Content View is unavoidable. The Content View can be distinguished from a thesis with stronger commitments, the Strong Content View, which is discussed toward the end of the chapter. Unlike the Strong Content View, which says that visual experience consists fundamentally in a propositional attitude, the Content View gives us a relatively neutral framework within which the Rich Content View can be assessed.

I first develop the Content View and discuss the notion of accuracy in section 2.1. Then, in section 2.2 I present an argument that apparently supports the Content View: the Argument from Accuracy. In section 2.3, I identify a flaw with this argument. In section 2.4, I present an argument for the Content View that corrects the flaw: the Argument from Appearing. In section 2.5, I consider two objections, each suggested by Charles Travis, concerning uses of *looks* and its cognates. These objections target the Argument from Accuracy, the Argument from Appearing, and the Content View itself. Finally, in section 2.6, I discuss the significance of the Content View and its status vis à vis Naïve Realism.

---

3. Martin (2002, 2004), Campbell (2002), Johnston (2006), and Brewer (2006) claim that Naïve Realism is incompatible with the Content View. Brewer argues that Berkeley would have opposed it, too.

2.1. CONTENTS AS ACCURACY CONDITIONS

It is common for philosophers to distinguish between veridical and non-veridical experiences. Descartes's evil-demon scenario is often described as a situation in which our experiences are not veridical. One might think that the Content View follows easily from the very idea that we sort experiences into the veridical and the non-veridical. If experiences can be veridical, it might be thought, then they have veridicality conditions, and if they have veridicality conditions, then they have contents, so the Content View is true.

   This argument does not sufficiently constrain what contents may be. For all the argument says, veridicality conditions may be like blueness conditions. A blueness condition is a condition that obtains exactly when something is blue. All blue things satisfy the same blueness condition: they are blue. If veridicality conditions are like blueness conditions, then all veridical experiences satisfy the same veridicality condition: they are veridical. If all there was to an experience's veridicality condition was being veridical, then veridicality conditions would not be very useful for defining contents, since all veridical experiences would have the same contents. A version of the Content View that entails that no two veridical experiences differ in their contents would not be worth defending. What's needed is a way to avoid this result.

   This result is avoided if contents are a kind of accuracy condition. To develop this idea, the Content View can be refined into a proposal that finds the following similarity between visual experiences and beliefs: like beliefs, maps, and newspapers, visual experiences have contents, and just as the contents of beliefs are conditions under which the belief state is true, so the contents of experiences are conditions under which the experience is accurate. According to this proposal, experiences are the kinds of states that can be accurate, and their contents are conditions under which they have this status. Just which accuracy conditions are contents of experience will be discussed in detail in the sections that follow. We can begin by focusing on accuracy itself.

If something is accurate, then there is something else in relation to which it is accurate.[4] If a map is accurate, then there is some spatial area in relation to which it is accurate. If a story about Simone is accurate in some respects but not others, then Simone has some of the features attributed to her by the story but not others. When a map, a story, a mental state, or anything else is accurate, there is a situation of which it is accurate. Attributing accuracy to something thus involves assessing it with respect to something else.

Let us focus on the case of episodic experiences (though the following points hold for maps, stories, and anything else that can be accurate or inaccurate). If an experience is inaccurate, then there is some mismatch between the experience and a situation. If there were no mismatch, the experience would be accurate. The conditions in which there is no mismatch are accuracy conditions. Analogous points hold for maps, stories, and other mental states besides experiences that can be accurate or inaccurate.

When we categorize token experiences as veridical (or veridical in certain respects), we are in the simplest case assessing them with respect to the situation in which they are had. If these classifications involve accuracy, then when we categorize an experience as veridical, we are saying that it is accurate with respect to this situation.

The Content View construes accuracy as freedom from error. When accuracy is construed in this way, the idea that accuracy comes in degrees can be understood by considering separate respects (such as location, color, or shape) in which an experience

4. This claim is compatible with deflationism about accuracy, where this is analogous to deflationism about truth. Even the deflationist about truth agrees that truth-apt sentences have truth conditions. Likewise, even the deflationist about accuracy can agree that if experiences can be accurate or inaccurate, then they have accuracy conditions.

is or is not accurate, and then breaking accuracy conditions down into separable contents. The Content View can thus respect the observation that accuracy comes in degrees. Completely accurate experiences would be ones in which all contents are true. Partly accurate experiences would be ones in which only some contents are true. For example, suppose experiences have contents, and consider an experience with the contents that there is a red cube in front of you, and a blue ball off to the left. If there really is a red cube in front of you and a ball off to the left, but the ball is black rather than blue, then your experience would be accurate with respect to the location of the ball, but inaccurate with respect to its color. It would be partly accurate, but inaccurate overall.[5]

5. When accuracy is construed as freedom from error, merely omitting truths about a situation will not by itself result in an inaccurate experience. A different notion of accuracy construes it as acuity, where greater acuity involves a higher degree of resolution. When accuracy is construed as acuity, the greater the degree to which an experience is accurate, the greater acuity the perceiver has, so that having microscopic eyes of the sort Locke and Leibniz discussed would yield relatively more accurate experiences, whereas having normal human eyes would yield relatively less accurate experiences (Locke [1689, book 2, chap. 12, sec. 14]). Cf. Leibniz: "If our eyes became better equipped or more penetrating, so that some colors or other qualities disappeared from our view, others would appear to arise out of them, and we should need a further increase in acuity to make them disappear too; and since matter is actually divided to infinity, this process could go on to infinity also." (New Essays on Human Understanding II.xxiii.12/Remmnant-Bennett, trans., p. 219).

In contrast to this notion of acuity, visual acuity is operationally defined in terms of ability to identify letters on a Snellen chart. At some levels of visual acuity, one might not reliably identify a Q (for instance, one might mistake it for an O), and that would be a misrepresentation at the level of belief—or if one is guessing, an erroneous guess. The standard notion of visual acuity does not take a stand on whether the errors that operationally define such low levels of acuity also occur at the level of experience. For all the operational definition says, experience may be neutral on the exact configuration of the letter's limbs (assuming that an individual letter can be made out at all), or it may misrepresent them.

In the case of belief, there are two things that can be true or false: the belief state, and the belief contents. Contrast the case of hope. If you hope that winter ends soon, your hope itself is neither true nor false, but the content that winter ends soon is. (Here the notion of content is not tied to accuracy conditions of a state, but simply to something that can be true or false.) According to the Content View, experiences are more like beliefs than hopes, in that they involve two things that can be free of error: the experience itself, and its content.

Given the construal of contents as accuracy conditions, we can distinguish between two aspects of experience that mirror the Fregean distinction between the force and sense of a sentence. An analogous distinction for mental states between their function and their content was drawn by the nineteenth-century German psychologists Carl Stümpf and Oswald Külpe in their discussions of perception and imagery.[6] To argue for the Content View, one has to show both that experiences (like hopes) involve relations to a relatum that can in turn be true or false, and also that experiences (unlike hopes) can themselves be accurate or inaccurate.

2.2 THE ARGUMENT FROM ACCURACY

We can now examine the first argument aimed at supporting the Content View. It resembles the argument with which we began in 2.1. But now we are armed with two additional ideas: contents are a kind of accuracy condition; and due to the nature of accuracy, accuracy conditions differ from blueness conditions, in that

6. On the distinction between force and Fregean sense, see Dummett (1981). Unlike Frege's notion of sense, Stümpf and Külpe's notion of content does not build in that contents are truth-evaluable. For discussion, see Boring (1929).

two experiences can be accurate yet differ in their accuracy conditions.

The Argument from Accuracy

P1: All experiences are accurate or inaccurate.
P2: If all experiences are accurate or inaccurate, then all experiences have accuracy conditions.
Conclusion: All experiences have accuracy conditions.

Let us examine each premise.

The Case for P1

Accuracy and inaccuracy are properties that a token experience would have relative to a situation: most naturally, the situation in which the experience is had. Later on, we will consider whether token experiences might be accurate or inaccurate with respect to other situations. For now we can take P1 to say that for all token experiences, there are some respects in which the experience is accurate or inaccurate relative to the situation in which it is had.

We can easily distinguish hallucinations and illusions from completely successful perceptions. Here are some examples:

Airport Hallucination: You are at home but hallucinate being in an airport.
Fishtank: The fish you are seeing is blue and it looks blue. It is at location L, but looks to be at location L*, which is a bit to the right of L.
Lunchtime: Behold your sandwich, cut in half on a plate. It is as it looks.

Although experiences such as *Airport Hallucination* probably never occur, we still find it easy to distinguish them from illusions and completely successful perceptions such as *Fishtank* and *Lunchtime*, which occur frequently. In a hallucination, perceptual contact is missing; illusions are misleading guides to what is in the environment. In contrast, completely successful perceptions typically lead to knowledge.[7] Experiences in this last group are often called *veridical*.

This distinction suggests the following defense of P1. When given certain descriptions pairing token experiences with the situations in which they are had, we easily classify them into these categories. The best explanation of these classifications is that the experiences classified as veridical are accurate (at least so far as the descriptions specify—further specification of the same experience in its situation could introduce inaccuracies), and experiences classified as illusions are inaccurate.

I will argue that this defense of P1 is basically correct. One might think that the argument is too simple, in light of further complications that arise once we distinguish between further varieties of veridicality. After drawing these further distinctions, I will defend P1 in a way that takes them into account.

Varieties of Veridicality

In addition to the distinction between *Fishtank, Lunchtime,* and *Airport Hallucination,* a related distinction between kinds of experiences is also natural for us to draw, even if we don't have labels in ordinary language that mark this difference. In that sense the distinction is pre-theoretical. It is illustrated by contrasting *Fishtank* with another experience, *Fishtank2:*

Fishtank: The fish you are seeing is blue and it looks blue. It is at location L, but looks to be at location L*, which is a bit to the right of L.
Fishtank2: The fish you are seeing is blue and at location L, and it looks blue and looks to be at L.

---

7. The stronger claim that completely successful perceptions always lead to knowledge seems false. There may be cases in which the cube's greenness plays the right role in producing the experience of seeing the cube, yet which do not lead to knowledge, either because the subject does not form any belief, or she does but has countervailing evidence against it, or some other necessary condition on knowledge is not met.

In *Fishtank*, there need be no illusion with respect to the fish's color or shape, but there is an illusion with respect to location. The experience is veridical with respect to color and shape, but not veridical with respect to location. It is thus partly but not completely veridical. In contrast, *Fishtank2* is completely veridical, so far as this experience is described.

Interestingly, hallucinations, too, can be veridical in some respects, and can differ from one another in their degree of veridicality:

> *Airport Hallucination:* You are at home but hallucinate being in an airport.
>
> *Amazing Coincidence:* Your experience is just as it is now, from your point of view, but you are hallucinating, and the scene before your eyes is nonetheless exactly as presented in your hallucination.

In one sense, *Airport Hallucination* is less veridical than *Amazing Coincidence*. But this sense of *veridical* differs from the sense of that word when it's used to label completely successful perceptions, as distinct from hallucinations and illusions, since *Airport Hallucination* and *Amazing Coincidence* are both hallucinations.

We can label the two uses of *veridical* as follows. Sometimes it is used to denote experiences that are veridical *of* the things seen. Call these experiences *strongly veridical*. Hallucinations cannot be strongly veridical. Other times, *veridical* is used to describe experiences that are veridical without being veridical of any object that is seen. For instance, through an amazing coincidence, a hallucination could occur in the presence of exactly the sort of scene that is hallucinated. Call *weakly veridical experiences* those that are veridical, whether or not they are strongly veridical.

Strongly veridical experiences may fall short of being completely successful. Completely successful experiences are best thought of as experiences in which the subject perceives both an object and its properties. Consider Simone, who systematically misperceives green things, so that to her green things look yellow. Suppose that by stimulating Simone's brain area V1 while she looked at a green cube, you accidentally induced in her an experience as of a green cube, when otherwise she would have an experience as of a yellow cube. The intervention does not correct Simone's systematic error. But on the basis of the experience that the intervention helps produce, it would be natural for Simone to form the true belief that there is a green cube before her. Intuitively, Simone's experience is not completely successful, because the greenness of the cube does not play the right role in producing the experience. Simone perceives the cube, and it looks green to her, but she does not perceive its greenness.[8]

Cases like this one are called *veridical illusion*.[9] They suggest that leading to true belief is not enough for complete success. In general, an experience will be completely successful if it is a case of seeing o when o looks F, o is F, and o's looking F is due to o's F-ness; that is, not to any irregular intervention. These experiences are not just strongly veridical, they are superstrongly veridical. They are cases of optimal perceptual contact with an object and select properties. The case of Simone illustrates how an experience could be accurate of an object the perceiver sees (and therefore strongly veridical) even if there is intuitively

8. For a similar case, see Johnston's discussion (2006) of the twins in the Ames room.
9. We can distinguish between two kinds of veridical illusion. The case of Simone illustrates *predicative* veridical illusions, which are strongly veridical even though intuitively, the experience is not completely successful. (For discussion of other cases in which something similar goes wrong, see Johnston [2006] and Smith [2010]). What seems to go wrong is that the perceiver's contact with the object's properties is suboptimal. In contrast to predicative visual illusions, *objectual* veridical illusions are veridical of an object distinct from the object that is seen, and so are weakly veridical without being strongly veridical. For instance, a red cube at location L^* looks orange and looks to be at location L, while hidden behind a mirror at location L there is an orange cube that otherwise looks exactly the way the red cube looks. So the experience is veridical of an orange cube, which is not seen by the perceiver, but is falsidical of the red cube, which the perceiver does see. A case with this structure is discussed by Grice (1961).

something missing from her perceptual contact with what she sees.

With the distinction between strong and weak veridicality in hand, we can see that the pre-theoretical distinction that was illustrated earlier between degrees of veridicality is not sensitive to whether experiences are strongly veridical (let alone superstrongly veridical). It is a distinction between degrees of weak veridicality. According to the straightforward account of what underlies our classification of experiences into partial and complete veridicality, weak veridicality is accuracy, and degrees of weak veridicality are degrees of accuracy. *Amazing Coincidence* is accurate with respect to the situation that the hallucinator is actually in, even though the hallucinator is not perceiving anything in that situation. If *Amazing Coincidence* represented that you were in a room containing yellow chairs, when in fact you were hallucinating while standing in a room containing red chairs, it would not be completely weakly veridical, but it could still be weakly veridical to a high degree.

How does the abductive defense of P1 fare in light of the complications introduced by veridical hallucinations and veridical illusions? Using the notion of weak veridicality, we can refine the defense as follows. When given certain descriptions pairing token experiences with situations in which they are had, such as *Fishtank, Fishtank2, Lunchtime, Airport Hallucination*, and *Amazing Coincidence*, we easily classify them into completely falsidical, partly veridical, or completely veridical (at least, completely veridical, for all the descriptions specify), where veridicality is weak veridicality. The best explanation of these classifications is that the experiences classified as completely veridical are completely accurate (so far as the descriptions specify), and experiences classified as partly veridical are only partly accurate.

What else might explain our classifications?

The abductive defense of P1 just described will not succeed if there are alternative, superior explanations of what underlies comparative classifications of *Fishtank* and *Fishtank2*, *Airport Hallucination*, and *Amazing Coincidence*, and our classification of some of these (*Fishtank*) as partly veridical, others (*Lunchtime*, *Fishtank2*, and *Amazing Coincidence*) as completely veridical, and still others (*Airport Hallucination*) as completely falsidical. The straightforward account has simplicity on its side. But let us consider the alternatives.

One might try to argue that the only classifications of accuracy in the vicinity are classifications of judgments downstream of experiences. This alternative will bring us straight to the heart of the controversy over the Content View, and it will be useful to have the second argument for the Content View on the table before exploring it. That argument—the Argument from Appearing—will be presented in section 2.4, and we'll return to the alternative explanation of our comparative classifications of experiences in section 2.5.

Another alternative is in the spirit of Naïve Realism, in that it attempts to define weak veridicality in terms of strong veridicality, or more generally in terms of the "good" case of experience. According to this alternative, the classifications are sensitive to a notion of weak veridicality that does not involve the notion of accuracy but instead involves the notion of indiscriminability from strongly veridical experiences. Such a notion of weak veridicality might be defined as follows:

> An experience is weakly veridical iff it is indiscriminable from a good case of perceiving something that has a cluster of properties F, and the experience is had by someone in the presence of something that has that cluster of properties.[10]

If properties are in a cluster, then if they are instantiated, they are all instantiated by the same thing. The cluster of properties F

---

10. Thanks to Adam Pautz for suggesting this proposal. Pautz (2009) considers the right-hand side of this proposal in a different dialectical context. He uses it to formulate a disjunctivist account of accuracy, which he draws on to argue that Naïve Realists can respect the standard classifications of experiences as accurate or inaccurate.

would have to be such that any two experiences that presented something as having F would be indistinguishable to the subject. Veridicality would then be partial if something is present with only some of the properties in the cluster; it would be complete if something is present with all the properties in the cluster.

On this proposal, a good case of perceiving something that has the cluster of properties F could be a strongly veridical experience as defined earlier (a case of perceiving the object and its properties), or it could be more strongly an experience that provides a basis for knowing that the object has those properties, or more strongly still, it could be a case of knowing that the object has those properties. No matter how the good case is defined, weak veridicality derives from the notion of the good case, which will be something like strong veridicality.

By itself, the status of weak veridicality as less fundamental than strong veridicality does not preclude experiences from being assessable for accuracy. Ultimately, this proposal does not seem to succeed in avoiding the notion of accuracy. Its right-hand side relies on the idea that there is a cluster of properties that an experience can either match or mismatch. According to the proposal, the status of an experience as weakly veridical depends on whether the cluster of properties that figures in the indiscriminability property is instantiated. An experience will be weakly veridical if and only if a cluster of properties is instantiated that matches the properties in the indiscriminability property. Little daylight can be found between this kind of matching and accuracy. Through the dependence of weak veridicality on this kind of match, the proposal reintroduces the notion of accuracy, rather than providing an alternative to it.[11]

11. The proposal faces another objection as well. Since weak veridicality is defined in terms of indiscriminability, which is in turn standardly defined in terms of knowledge (Williamson 1990; Martin 2004, 2006), it appears that cognitively unsophisticated creatures cannot count as having strongly veridical experiences. (More specifically, if a mental state cannot provide a basis for knowledge in a creature that isn't capable of

And from this fact we can draw an important moral: the claim that experiences can be accurate or inaccurate can be true, even if the assessability of an experience for accuracy is less fundamental than its status as a "good" case of perception.

The Case for P2

So far, we have defended the first premise in the Argument from Accuracy. The second premise is P2.

> P2: If all experiences are accurate or inaccurate, then all experiences have accuracy conditions.

There are two routes to P2. First, P2 is true on the simple grounds that accuracy (like blueness) is a property, and so if all experiences are the kinds of things that can be accurate or inaccurate, then there will be conditions under which experiences are accurate. From P1 and P2, it follows that all experiences have accuracy conditions. The first route to P1 yields accuracy conditions that obtain only when the experience occurs. In contrast, the second route to P2 yields accuracy conditions that may obtain even when the experience does not occur. P2 is true if experiences can be assessed for accuracy with respect to situations other than those in which they are had. And it is plausible to think that they can be so assessed. Recall the cases described earlier:

> *Fully Falsidical Hallucination:* You are at home but are hallucinating being in an airport.
>
> *Fully Amazing Coincidence:* You hallucinate being in an airport, and you are in an airport. The scene before your eyes is exactly as presented in your hallucination.
>
> *Less Amazing (but still pretty amazing) Coincidence:* You hallucinate being in an airport, and you are in an airport that is exactly like the one you're hallucinating in some but not all respects.

---

knowledge, then it seems that such creatures can't have strongly veridical experiences.) This objection is developed in Siegel (2004). See also Byrne and Logue (2008), Farkas (2006), Hawthorne and Kovakovich (2006), Pautz (2010), and Sturgeon (2006).

These cases describe pairs of hallucinations and the situations in which they are had. But we can also fix on the first hallucination (*Fully Falsidical Hallucination*) as an anchor point, and think of the other cases as counterfactual situations relative to which we can evaluate the original hallucination. For the purposes of evaluating the original hallucination in this way, we can just ignore the experiences that occur in the two Amazing Coincidences, and consider the extent to which they are situations that match the original hallucination. Relative to the Less Amazing but still pretty amazing situation, the original hallucination would be more veridical than it is in the original case (when you are at home). Relative to the Fully Amazing situation, the original hallucination would be even more veridical.

We reach these verdicts concerning veridicality on the basis of information about what conditions obtain in the counterfactual situation. In general, suppose we evaluate an experience (such as *Fully Falsidical Hallucination*) with respect to a situation other than the one in which it is had. Call this situation world w. We will count the experience as veridical with respect to w only when properties are instantiated in w that are presented in the experience.[12] This kind of assessment does not trivially require the presence of an experience. The conditions are veridicality conditions that can be satisfied in worlds where the experience does not occur.

2.3. A FLAW IN THE ARGUMENT FROM ACCURACY

Considered as a defense of the Content View, the Argument from Accuracy is not good enough. Nothing in the argument tells us that the accuracy conditions are fit to be contents. This flaw is

12. On the plausible assumption that visual phenomenology presents spatial features such as being nearby the perceiver (considered as the center), we will count an experience as veridical with respect to a centered world only when such features are instantiated in it.

especially vivid on the first route to P2. If I see a red cube and my experience of seeing it is accurate, one of the conditions that obtains exactly when my experience is accurate is the condition that my experience is accurate. For all the Argument from Accuracy says, this condition is included in the accuracy conditions had by experiences. But it may be implausible to suppose that this accuracy condition is a content, depending on the conception of contents. If contents are sets of possible worlds, then this accuracy condition may be equivalent to more substantive ones, but on other conceptions it would be distinct. If it is distinct, it is intuitively not conveyed to the subject. This potentially silly kind of accuracy condition is in some ways analogous to a blueness condition, in that it is shared by all accurate experiences just as the blueness condition (bluenesss) is shared by all blue objects. Yet nothing in the argument from accuracy rules it out as a content of experience.

In reply, one might point out that the potentially silly kind of accuracy condition is avoided by the second route to P2, in which experiences can be assessed for accuracy with respect to situations other than those in which they are had. Accuracy conditions that can be satisfied in worlds where the experience does not occur will not include the condition that the experience is accurate, as they do not require the presence of the experience at all.

But even this defense of P2 leaves the Argument from Accuracy with the same general flaw. The flaw is that the argument does not tell us whether the accuracy conditions had by experiences are suitable for being contents of experience, given the constraint that contents are conveyed to the subject by her experience. What needs support is not just the generic conclusion that experiences have any old accuracy conditions, but the more robust conclusion that they have accuracy conditions that are conveyed to the subject. The mere fact that the accuracy conditions we get from the second route to P2 (i.e., those defined over worlds in which the experience does not occur) avoid the potentially silly accuracy condition does not by itself ensure that the rest of the accuracy conditions are conveyed. And it could turn out that some accuracy conditions defined only over worlds where the experience does occur *are* conveyed (the potentially silly accuracy condition mentioned earlier—the condition that the experience is accurate—is not the only condition that can be so defined). Thus, distinguishing between the two routes to P2 brings us no closer to the heart of the matter.[13] The general flaw with the Argument from Accuracy is that it is not an argument for the Content View as contents have been defined here. A good argument for the Content View should tie together accuracy conditions and contents, elucidating why experiences are assessable for accuracy in the first place, and how they could convey their accuracy conditions to the subject.

2.4. THE ARGUMENT FROM APPEARING

We can find such elucidation in the Argument from Appearing. This argument attempts to unearth the idea that experiences are assessable for accuracy, aiming to explain what gives them accuracy conditions that are suitable for being contents, thereby bridging the gap between accuracy conditions and contents. It does this by starting with something that is conveyed to the subject, out of which accuracy conditions fit to be contents can be built.

The Argument from Appearing proceeds from premises about the phenomenal character of visual perceptual experience. The accuracy conditions that figure in its conclusion derive from the properties that are presented in visual phenomenology. Premise (i) claims that properties are presented in visual phenomenology, premise (ii) links these properties to instantiation at a world, which is in turn linked to accuracy conditions in premises (iii) and (iv).

13. At least, it doesn't bring us any closer, absent a good account of why accuracy conditions defined over worlds where the experience does not occur are always conveyed. If there were such an account, the Argument from Appearing would not be needed.

THE ARGUMENT FROM APPEARING

Premise (i)
All visual perceptual experiences present clusters of properties as being instantiated.

Premise (ii)
If an experience E presents a cluster of properties F as being instantiated, then:
Necessarily: things are the way E presents them only if property-cluster F is instantiated.

Premise (iii)
If necessarily: things are the way E presents them only if property-cluster F is instantiated, then:
E has a set of accuracy conditions C, conveyed to the subject of E, such that:
C is satisfied in a world only if there is something that has F in that world.

Premise (iv)
If E has a set of accuracy conditions C, conveyed to the subject of E, such that E is accurate only if C, then:
E has a set of accuracy conditions C^*, conveyed to the subject of E, such that E is accurate iff C^*.

Conclusion: All visual perceptual experiences have contents.

The general strategy of the argument is to reason about an arbitrary visual perceptual experience, E, and then draw a conclusion about all visual perceptual experiences.

Premise (i)

According to Premise (i), all visual perceptual experiences present clusters of properties as being instantiated. Is this description of experiences phenomenologically apt?

Typically, our visual perceptual experiences are cases of seeing objects, where the category of objects includes ordinary objects such as cars, cups, and pencils.[14] Why think that properties are presented in such experiences? Consider the claim (made sometimes in discussions of metaphysics) that there is no such thing as a "bare particular"—that is, an object shorn of all of its properties.[15] Premise (i) is motivated by the idea that it is not possible for us to represent objects as so shorn in our visual experience. When we see (or even when we merely seem to see) ordinary objects, such as a cube, bare particulars do not figure in visual phenomenology in any way. Properties enter the picture as well. For you to see a cube at all, it must be part of your visual phenomenology that the cube has certain properties: having a certain number of facing edges and surfaces, having a certain color, location, and so on.

14. The category should also be taken to include "Spelke-objects"—roughly, things that can survive radical changes in kind but are bounded, capable of continuous motion (and not of discontinuous motion), and are not parts of other objects. There is debate among psychologists concerning what principles of individuation govern perceptual representations of objects. (For discussion, see essays in Scholl [2002] and Dickie [2011]). A similar question could be raised specifically about visual phenomenology. Does visual phenomenology ever attribute properties to Spelke-objects, or is it neutral on the status of objects as Spelke-objects or ordinary objects? (The answer will probably vary between infants and adults.) It won't matter for the Argument from Appearing how this question about visual phenomenology is answered, as accuracy conditions of the sort described in (iii) can be defined on any of these construals of objects. But the answer will bear on which accuracy conditions experiences have.

15. As bare particulars are defined here, they are objects without properties. Bare particulars thus should not be identified with the substrata recognized by opponents of the bundle theory. Substrata are not meant to be (even potentially) bare particulars in the present sense. The debate between proponents of substrata and proponents of the bundle theory concerns whether denying the bundle theory forces you into saying that there are bare particulars in the present sense. For discussion, see Locke (1689), Martin (1980), and Sider (2006).

Most of the time, visual phenomenology takes a stand on which objects instantiate clusters of properties, both at a time and over time.[16] For instance, when you see a bird flying by, it looks as if a single object is moving. Your experience does not remain neutral on whether it is the same object at various points along the trajectory. But in some cases, an experience may present the perceiver with a property without specifying what is instantiating it. For instance, Dretske (1999) discusses the case in which you can't tell whether the moving train is the one you're seeing or the one you're sitting in. Even here, though, this is part of a visual experience that does attribute properties to objects.[17]

We thus see objects, and we can't seem to see them without our experience presenting them as having certain properties. It should be noted that premise (i) can be read *de dicto* or *de re*, depending on the relative scope of "presentation" and "properties." I've been assuming the *de re* reading, on which for each visual perceptual experience, there are some properties (color, relative location, etc.) such that the experience presents those properties as instantiated. On the *de dicto* reading, in contrast, each visual perceptual experience presents it as being the case that some properties are instantiated, but given an experience *E* there need be no specific properties such that *E* presents them as instantiated. At first glance it might be hard to see how the *de dicto* reading could be phenomenologically apt, given the main idea that the properties characterize how things look to the perceiver. But if one adds another moving part to the equation, such as a mode of presentation of a property, the *de dicto* reading can

16. Clark (2000) suggests that visual phenomenology presents us only with properties instantiated at locations ("feature-placing"), without taking a stand on which objects are instantiating the properties. The objection that this is phenomenally inadequate in cases of perceived motion can be found in Siegel (2002). Clark (2004) makes explicit that visual phenomenology is not limited to feature-placing.
17. Dretske (1999). Unlike Clark (2000), Dretske accepts that properties are sometimes attributed to objects in experience.

begin to look more plausible. Modes of presentation will be discussed in connection with premise (iv), by which time it will be easier to assess their impact on the Argument from Appearing. For now, more can be said about how properties figure in experience, whether we read premise (i) *de dicto* or *de re*.

Suppose you see a cube, and it looks red and cubical. Here your experience presents it as being the case that there is a red cube before you. Contrast a hope that there is a red cube in front of you. The properties of being red and cubical figure in the content of the hope. But in hoping that there is a red cube in front of you, it need not be presented to you as being the case that there is a red cube in front of you. To make this vivid, suppose your eyes are closed, and you're not holding onto anything or engaging in any visual imagination. Under such circumstances you could still hope that when you open your eyes there will be a red cube in front of you. In contrast, when such a property cluster (redness, cubicality, and being nearby) figures in visual perceptual experience, the experience presents it as being the case that a red cube is nearby. It is the fact that properties figure in this way that will eventually allow us to draw the link to accuracy conditions of the state, rather than merely the contents.

These considerations about the kind of visual phenomenology involved in seeing ordinary objects support premise (i), and they apply equally to cases of merely seeming to see objects.[18] The same considerations also suggest that a sense of *looks* and *appears* can be defined in which, when you see an object, it looks (appears) to you to have properties. (We will revisit this suggestion for defining a sense of *looks* in section 2.5.)

It should be taken as analytic that if an experience presents a property as being instantiated, then it presents the property as being instantiated by something other than the experience itself.

---

18. Hallucinations that are indiscriminable from perception are not cases of seeing to see a bare particular, nor of seeming to see properties that are not instantiated by anything.

For all premise (i) says (and, indeed, for all the Content View says), there may be more to the phenomenal character of an experience than what it presents. For instance, premise (i) allows that experiences present themselves as having non-relational properties, such as being blurred. In some accounts of blurred vision (e.g., Smith [2008], Pace [2007]), part of what is presented (in a broader sense than the one used here) to the subject by her blurred experience is that her vision is blurred. Our more restrictive notion is compatible with treatments of blurred vision such as Smith's, but it is better suited than the broader notion to being linked to accuracy conditions.[19]

Premise (ii)

(ii) If an experience E presents a cluster of properties F as being instantiated, then:
  Necessarily: things are the way E presents them only if property-cluster F is instantiated.

Premise (ii) is an instance of a more general claim about presentation that is independently plausible: if a state presents such-and-such as being the case, then things are the way the state presents them only if such-and-such. The general claim seems plausible, no matter what presentation is. But to bring the general claim into focus, it may be useful to discuss the notion of presenting such-and-such as being the case a bit further.[20] Other mental states

---

19. Premise (i) is at odds with a view explored by Sturgeon (2006, 2008) and defended by Fish (2008, 2009), according to which hallucinations don't have any phenomenal character at all. If hallucinations lack phenomenal character altogether, then (assuming they are nonetheless visual perceptual experiences), they will be counterexamples to (i). The idea that hallucinations lack phenomenal character is at odds with the crudest deliverances of introspection. Fish's proposal is discussed and criticized in Siegel (2008).

20. Searle (1983) discusses a closely related category of mental states, called "Bel-states," of which belief is supposed to be a paradigm. For

besides experiences can present things as being the case, and some states can do this without involving any phenomenal character, though (ii) would be just as plausible, even if presentation were tied specifically to phenomenal character. For instance, belief and supposition are modes in which things may be presented as being the case. The kind of commitment involved in belief is a specific kind of presentation, but not the only kind, as it is missing in supposition and imagination. My supposition that it will not rain tomorrow presents it as being the case that it will not rain tomorrow, but my supposition does not involve the same kind of commitment as belief.

Premises (iii) and (iv)

Like premise (ii), premises (iii) and (iv) are closely related to more general claims. Without the conveying constraint, these premises follow from more general claims, and these claims are independent of any claims about phenomenology. Consider premise (iii) without the conveying constraint:

(iii-minus-conveying-constraint) If necessarily: things are the way E presents them only if property-cluster F is instantiated, then:
   E has a set of accuracy conditions C such that:
      C is satisfied in a world only if there is something that has F in that world.

Searle the defining feature of Bel-states is their mind-to-world direction of fit, which is in turn illustrated using the metaphor that it is the "fault" of the world, not the mind, if the Bel-state is not satisfied (1983, p. 7). Once we stop relying on the metaphor, the notion of mind-to-world direction of fit seems best understood as a norm to the effect that beliefs should be adjusted to fit the evidence, and evidence should not be gerrymandered to match antecedently formed beliefs. But this understanding of mind-to-world direction of fit is not useful to delimiting any class of mental states that includes experiences, since unlike beliefs, experiences are not the kinds of states that can be supported by evidence.

This claim follows from an independently plausible more general thesis:

> If things are the way that a state X presents them as being only if conditions C obtain, then X has accuracy conditions that are satisfied in a world only if C obtains.

Given that premise (iii) without the conveying constraint follows from this independently plausible thesis, our question should be whether once we add the conveying constraint we end up with accuracy conditions that meet this constraint. Are accuracy conditions that derive from properties presented in experience conveyed to the subject?

We can distinguish between three ways in which a content can be conveyed to the subject by her experience. First, a content is conveyed by experience if it would be a content of explicit beliefs that are natural to form on the basis of visual experience.[21] Second, a content is conveyed to the subject by her experience if it enables the experience to guide bodily actions. For instance, suppose you see the door but don't form any explicit beliefs about the shape of its doorknob, yet you adjust your grip in advance of touching the doorknob as you reach for it. This could be a case of visual experience guiding action. Finally, a content is conveyed to the subject by her experience if it is manifest to introspection that it is a content of experience.

If there are properties presented in visual phenomenology, this opens the possibility that since those properties are conveyed to

---

21. According to some philosophers, potential contents of visual experience are so fundamentally different from potential contents of beliefs that it is impossible to believe exactly what you experience, and so the contents of experiences could not be conveyed to the subject in this first sense. They could, however, be conveyed in a similar sense, if there was a systematic relationship between experience contents and belief contents. Providing such an account would need to be done anyway in order to describe the differences between beliefs that are closer to the deliverances of perception and those that are farther removed from it. For discussion, see Heck (2007).

the subject, the accuracy conditions they directly determine are also so conveyed. What would it be for a property presented in experience to be conveyed to the subject by her experience? In cases of seeing objects, properties that are presented in visual phenomenology are properties that objects look to the perceiver to have when she sees them. Such properties can be conveyed to the subject in the same ways that the contents of an experience can be conveyed to a subject. And there is good reason to think that such properties are conveyed in these ways. For instance, upon seeing the banana, it is natural to believe that it is yellow and bent, and this is arguably because those properties (being yellow, being bent) are presented in visual phenomenology.[22] Similarly, upon seeing the doorknob, it is natural for one's active movements to adjust to what one sees, as when you automatically adjust your grip to match its shape.[23] Finally, it seems manifest to introspection that visual phenomenology presents spatial properties (such as being nearby or in front of the perceiver), color properties (or properties closely related to colors), and shape and luminance properties—though it is doubtful that for every property presented in visual phenomenology, it is manifest to introspection that it is so represented.[24]

22. Cf. Logue (2009). Since we bring plenty of standing representations to bear on perceptual beliefs, one can't infer from the fact that one believes that (say) somebody is Franco that the property of being Franco is presented in visual phenomenology. But what is at issue here are inferences in the other direction: if a property is presented in visual phenomenology, then it is natural to attribute that property to something one sees.

23. The Ebbinghaus illusion suggests that action is also guided by visual representations of properties that do not figure in visual phenomenology. The claim of interest here is not that if action is guided by a visual representation of some properties, then those properties figure in visual phenomenology. Rather, the claim is that if properties are presented in visual phenomenology, then they may be fit to guide action.

24. Discovering which properties figure in experience is difficult, and in many cases introspectively reflecting on an experience does little to

Supposing that properties presented in experience are conveyed to the subject, does this support the idea that accuracy conditions that derive directly from those properties are so conveyed? It is hard to see how such accuracy conditions could fail to be conveyed to the subject in whatever way the properties they derive from are. If it is natural to believe that the banana is yellow when it looks yellow because the property of yellowness is conveyed to the subject by her experience, then the content that something is yellow will be conveyed as well. Likewise, if the property F-ness is presented in experience and guides one's action, then this seems enough for the content that something is F to guide one's action.

Premise (iv) also follows from an independently plausible general thesis, when divorced from the conveying constraint.

(iv-minus-conveying-constraint): If there are some conditions C such that E is accurate only if C, then:
there are some conditions C^* such that E is accurate iff C^*.

In general, it is plausible that whenever there are some conditions C such that X is accurate only if C (where X is any kind of mental state), there are some (perhaps stronger) conditions C^* such that X is accurate iff C^*. Once the conveying constraint is added in, is the resulting premise true? In effect, our question is whether E has "iff"-accuracy conditions that are conveyed to the subject. Can the "only-if" conditions of premise (iii) be turned into "iff"-contents?

Premise (iii) remains plausible once "only if" is replaced by "iff." But for this replacement to preserve the argument's force, "only if" would have to be replaced by "iff" in premise (ii) as well. A version of premise (ii) with "iff" would be true only given the

---

help one decide whether a property is presented in visual phenomenology, or farther downstream. For example, introspection alone does not seem to tell us whether visual phenomenology presents an object as Franco (and so not as his twin), or as someone with certain facial features that Franco's twin could equally share, or as merely a human-shaped entity that a non-human alien could equally share.

assumption that what an experience E presents as being the case is exhausted by E's presenting certain properties as instantiated. And here two complications arise that could raise the suspicion that iff-accuracy conditions for experience cannot be derived from the only-if accuracy condition stated in premise (iii). The first complication concerns the role of objects that we see in accuracy conditions, and the second concerns whether there are conditions on accuracy other than properties. To quell the suspicion, what's needed are reasons to think that these complications present no bar to defining full iff-accuracy conditions that are fit to be contents.

WHAT ABOUT OBJECTS?

Suppose you see Franco, and your experience represents him as sitting down. In order for the experience to be accurate with respect to a world, does Franco himself have to be sitting down in that world, or is it enough for accuracy if a qualitative duplicate of Franco is sitting down in that situation? For instance, is your experience veridical with respect to a world where Franco's twin is sitting down but Franco is standing up?

As they stand, the "only-if" versions of (ii) and (iii) leave unsettled whether accuracy conditions track objects seen across worlds, since they do not specify which object has to instantiate the cluster of properties F, in order for the experience of seeing that object to be accurate. To get a full definition of accuracy conditions, this issue must be settled.

But whichever way the issue is settled, the resulting accuracy conditions are fit to be contents of experience. If you see Franco and your experience represents him as sitting down, it is natural to believe on the basis of your experience that Franco is sitting down. It is also natural to believe that someone with a certain appearance is sitting down. These are both ways for contents to be conveyed to a subject. So both options result in accuracy conditions that have a good claim to being conveyed to the subject by her experience.[25]

WHY PROPERTIES? FREGEAN CONTENTS, CENTERED WORLDS AND TROPES

The assumption that what an experience E presents as being the case is exhausted by E's presenting certain properties as instantiated is called into question by scenarios in which it seems prima facie that two perceivers accurately represent different properties, yet have experiences that are phenomenally the same. Objects typically look to stand in certain spatial relations to the perceiver, such as being nearby or within reach. On some views (e.g., Egan [2006, 2010]), this involves the presentation of "centering features" defined in terms of evaluation in centered worlds. For example, in contrast to *being nearby Susanna*, which is a property, the centering feature *being nearby the center* is not a property, since being a center is merely a formal feature of a centered world. The claim that centering features are presented in experience is motivated by the idea that pairs of veridical phenomenally identical experiences can nonetheless be associated with different locations, and thus convey different contents.

Centering features provide a level at which such phenomenally identical experiences present the same thing. Fregean modes of presentation have been invoked to play a similar role in response to inversion scenarios. In spectral inversion, phenomenally identical pairs of veridical color experiences are associated with different color properties. In one such scenario, Invert's and

25. In chapter 6, the distinction between strong and weak veridicality will figure in an argument that an experience could have both kinds of accuracy conditions.

Nonvert's color experiences are phenomenally the same, but
Invert's experience presents red while Nonvert's experience
presents green. Is the phenomenal similarity between Invert and
Nonvert a mere "raw feel," or does it have some other status?
Chalmers (2004) argues that Invert and Nonvert's shared phenomenal character covaries with a level of content that is composed of
Fregean modes of presentation, where these are part of a two-
dimensionalist theory of experience content. (Thompson [2010]
defends a similar two-dimensionalist theory on the basis of inversion scenarios involving spatial properties.)[26]

A version of premise (ii) with "iff" would be true only given the
assumption that what an experience E presents as being the case
is exhausted by E's presenting certain properties as instantiated.
But this assumption is false if experience presents centering features rather than properties, or in addition to them. A modified
version of the argument could deal with this issue, however, by
replacing references to properties by references to features (properties or centering features), and by replacing references to worlds
by reference to centered worlds. So this obstacle to defining "iff"
accuracy conditions is easily overcome.

A similar dialectic surrounds two-dimensionalist Fregean
views. On these views, even if the contents of an experience E

26. Both the two-dimensionalist Fregean theory of experience content
and the theory that experiences present centering features suggest an
objection to premise (i): when you see objects, they look to have features
that are not properties, such as centering features or modes of presentation. However, this objection to premise (i) can be met, since centering
features and modes of presentation could be presented in experience
along with the location and color properties with which they are associated. Indeed, each of these theoretical devices is invoked to explain the
means by which such properties are presented in experience. Premise (i)
does not entail that any pair of phenomenally identical experiences present exactly the same properties. In addition, both the view that experiences present centering features and the Fregean views about experience
are versions of the Content View, and so do not ultimately challenge the
conclusion of the Argument from Appearing.

derive from what E presents as being the case, what experiences present as being the case is not exhausted by the instantiation of properties, because properties are presented under a mode of presentation that can pick out different properties in different worlds. For instance, according to Chalmers and Thompson, the mode of presentation for redness (roughly, "the property normally causing reddish experiences in me") picks out different properties in different worlds. These theories allow that two experiences could present redness as being instantiated, yet differ in the mode of presentation of redness, and hence in their accuracy conditions.

It is possible to formulate versions of (ii) and (iii) that would accommodate these two-dimensionalist Fregean views, on which accuracy conditions are determined by modes of presentation of properties.[27] In effect these theories posit two sets of accuracy conditions for experience: one set that covaries with phenomenal character (found at the level of sense or modes of presentation),

27. Premises (ii) and (iii) might be reformulated to accommodate two-dimensionalist Fregean views as follows:

2D Fregean (ii)
If an experience E presents a cluster of properties F as being instantiated, then:
> Necessarily: things in world w are the way E presents them only if something in w has a cluster of properties that meet the conditions on extension that F meets in the world where E occurs.

2D Fregean (iii)
If necessarily: things in world w are the way E presents them only if something in w has a cluster of properties that meet the conditions on extension that F meets in the world where E occurs, then:
> E has a set of accuracy conditions C, conveyed to the subject of E, such that:
>> C is satisfied in a world w only if something in w has a cluster of properties that meet the conditions on extension that F meets in the world E occurs.

and the other set that does not (found at the level of reference or properties presented in experience). When coupled with two-dimensional theories of belief, both sets of accuracy conditions in experience will be conveyed to the subject, to the extent that they each have an analog in the contents of beliefs formed on the basis of experience.[28]

Finally, one might think that it is tropes rather than universals that are presented in experiences, and that ultimately figure in their accuracy conditions. The Argument from Appearing could easily be reformulated to accommodate this position. In the reformulation, "tropes" could be substituted for "properties," except the consequent of premise (ii) would read "things are the way E's visual phenomenology presents them only if a cluster of F tropes is instantiated." For instance, F might be a cluster of red-cubical tropes, where a type of trope is determined by a primitive resemblance relation between tropes.[29]

28. A potential dialectical difficulty might remain. To defend a version of the Argument from Appearing that included 2D Fregean (ii) and (iii), what would be needed are reasons to accept these premises that do not antecedently assume the Content View. The defenses of Fregean contents given by Chalmers and Thompson take the Content View for granted. They argue that the Fregean contents are needed to make the right predictions about the veridicality of experiences involving inversion with respect to color and spatial features. (Thompson [2006] also argues that his contents are needed to make the right predictions about color constancy.) Perhaps related considerations about these phenomena could be used to support 2D Fregean (ii) and (iii) in footnote 27 without assuming the Content View.

29. A trope version of (iii) would look like this:

If necessarily: things are the way E presents them only if a cluster of F-tropes is instantiated, then:
   E has a set of accuracy conditions C, conveyed to the subject of E, such that:
      C is satisfied in a world only if there is something that has a cluster of F-tropes in that world.

2.5 TWO OBJECTIONS FROM *LOOKS, APPEARS,* AND THEIR COGNATES

Premise (i) of the Argument from Appearing, like the descriptions given earlier of *Airport, Fishtank, Fishtank 2, Lunchtime,* etc., all use *look, present,* or cognates. Without relying on descriptions like these, the argument could not get off the ground. I will now consider a pair of objections to such uses of *look* and its cognates. The second objection in the pair brings us to the heart of the controversy over the Content View.

According to the first objection, there are no natural uses of English words *look, visually present,* or their cognates that pick out contents of experience exclusively. Call this the semantic objection:

Semantic Objection

No actual uses of *looks* (or *looks F*) and its cognates in ordinary English exclusively track what is presented in experience.

The discussion so far has relied on the idea that we can use ordinary English expressions (including such locutions as *looks F*) to identify visual perceptual experiences, as opposed to mental states further downstream of perception. According to a specific version of the semantic objection, the only mental states that can be picked out by ordinary English uses of *looks F* and *looks to be F* are judgments that it would be reasonable to make on the basis of experience. If that is true, then the putative descriptions of experiences used in arguing for P1 of the Argument from Accuracy and in discussing premise (iii) of the Argument from Appearing are defective. Similarly, the Argument from Appearing uses the phrase "experience presents clusters of properties," and in cases where the experience is a case of seeing an object, the properties presented are meant to be properties that the object looks to the perceiver to have. So the Argument from Appearing depends on the idea that objects look to have properties—and here again the English expressions *looks F* and *looks to be F* are indispensable.

Something close to the semantic objection seems to be in play in Travis (2004). Travis raises doubts that any actual uses of *looks* in English report contents of visual perceptual experience. His official target is the idea that "the representational content of an experience can be read off of the way, in it, things looked." He says he will "begin to examine that idea by distinguishing and exploring two different notions of looks," and that "neither . . . makes room for it." (69).[30]

The first notion of looks is characterized by Travis as follows:

> On the first notion, something looks thus-and-so, or like such-and-such, where it looks the way such-and-such . . . does (would) might look. On this notion, Pia may look . . . like . . . her sister. . . . That man on the bench looks old. (He looks the way an old man would or might).[31]

In a footnote, Travis makes explicit that public looks—which can be expressed by the locutions "looking like X" or "looking F"—are supposed to contrast with looking like X or looking F to a

---

30. Although Travis sets out to attack the idea that experiences have "representational content," the characterizations offered of the official target is more restricted than standard characterizations of the view. First, the target holds that contents can be "read off" of the ways things look. Substituting "phenomenal character" for "the ways things look" would result in the view that for any two experiences with the same phenomenal character, there is some content that both share. But some proponents of the idea that experiences have content deny this—such as Block (1996), who argues that that there are pairs of experiences that have the same phenomenal character but differ in their content. Second, substituting "known by introspection alone" for "read off" results in the claim that introspection can tell us what contents experiences have. This claim is not entailed by the Content View, and I argue against it in chapter 3. A wider target for Travis (and one that would make his criticisms more powerful) would look to constraints on contents by phenomenal character, without endorsing the supervenience claim, and without importing the assumption that we can discover what contents experiences have using introspection alone.

31. Travis (2004, 70).

perceiver.[32] Travis sometimes calls looks on the first construal "demonstrable looks."[33] His main criticism is that demonstrable looks don't fix on any single way the world has to be, in order for an experience to be accurate. Travis takes the question facing his opponent to be: what way does something have to be, in order to be the way that it demonstrably looks?[34] If there are conflicting ways a thing could be in order to be the way it demonstrably looked, then, Travis concludes, contents of experience cannot be read off of demonstrable looks.

Travis thinks this is just what we find.[35] A lemon, a lemon-shaped and colored soap, a small football in a lemon disguise, and countless other things could all share a demonstrable lemony look. How does the lemon (or the disguised football, etc.) have to be in order to be the way it looks? You might think the answer is: it has to be yellowish and roughly lemon-shaped. But there are many lemony demonstrable looks, not all of which involve being yellowish and lemon-shaped. Maybe the lemon is cut in half. Maybe it's got a green patch. So a lemony demonstrable look seems too coarsely grained an item to determine any set of contents for experience. Alternatively, you might think the answer is: it has to be a lemon. But that may seem arbitrary: why a lemon, as opposed to a football in disguise, or a well-crafted yellow soap? Even if we fix on a specific lemony demonstrable look that pins

32. Travis (2004, footnote 12).

33. Cf. Ginet (1975, chap. 5).

34. Travis (2004, 71): "If perception is representational, then for any perceptual experience, there must be a way things are according to it . . . things looking as they do on a given occasion must fix what representational content experience then has."

35. "Things looking . . . as they do fixes no way things should be to be the way they look full stop. . . . There is just too much things look like . . . in having the demonstrable looks they do" (Travis 2004, 78–79). Cf. Travis (2004, 74): "The conclusion so far is that on our first notion of looks, looking like such-and-such cannot contribute to determining how things should be to be the way they look simpliciter. For so far as it goes, there is no particular way things should be to be the way they look simpliciter."

down shape, color, and illumination, we still don't seem to fix on any set of truth conditions. Finally, you might think the answer is: once you fix a specific lemony demonstrable look, for something to be the way it demonstrably looks, it has to have just those properties that are involved in fixing the specific lemony demonstrable look: as it might be, lemon-shaped, roughly textured, yellowish, and so on.

Of these three answers to Travis's question, the third seems the most sensible, as far as it goes. But whatever status the answers may have, the question itself seems flawed, driven as it is by the idea that demonstrable looks might fix contents of experience. If the fact that a lemon demonstrably looks lemony doesn't entail that it looks lemony to S, why should we think that the lemon's demonstrable looks fix the facts about the contents of S's experience when she sees the lemon? At best these facts are fixed by S's experience somehow picking up the demonstrable look of the lemon, when she sees it. But with the notion of *picking up on* a demonstrable look, we've introduced another kind of looking altogether. Demonstrable looks are irrelevant to fixing the content of experience. Since they are public, they are part of the way the world is, and as such don't automatically determine how the world looks, appears, seems, or is presented to a perceiver. If any notion of looking is going to constrain the contents of experience, it must be looking some way to a perceiver.[36]

36. The second construal of "looking" that Travis considers is also a notion of public looks, and so likewise does not directly challenge the Argument from Appearing, or more generally the idea that the phenomenal character of an experience constrains its contents. The second notion is expressed by locutions that begin with "It looks as if . . ." and take an indicative propositional complement, such as "It looks as if Pia will sink the putt" (or "It looks like Pia will sink the putt"—these are Travis's examples). Like demonstrable looks, these (putative) facts are also supposed to be public facts about how things look, rather than facts about mental states; Travis writes: "It cannot look as if X on this notion where it is perfectly plain that X is not so" (2004, 76). It might be "perfectly plain"

Suppose we grant that *looks* and its cognates as actually used in English do not exclusively track what's presented in visual phenomenology. This could be true, even if there was a special, regimented sense of *looks* that did track what's presented in visual phenomenology, yet bears enough resemblance to ordinary uses to make it reasonable to choose the English word for that purpose.[37] For the objection to have any force against the Content View, what's needed is reason to think that there couldn't be any such regimented use that could figure in the Argument from Appearing when it uses the notion of visual phenomenology presenting properties to a subject. We can thus distinguish the semantic objection from a more powerful objection, according to which no such regimentation is possible. Call this the psychological objection:

Psychological Objection

There is no mental state for any uses of *looks F* and its cognates to track, other than judgments that would be reasonable to make on the basis of experience.

If the psychological objection stands, then we can explain why we make the comparative classifications of veridicality in cases such as *Fishtank, Airport,* and the other cases described in section 2.2 without relying on the idea that experiences themselves are

---

that the sphere is to the right of a green cube, while nonetheless looking as if it is alone on the table to someone who is blind in their right visual field. If "it looks as if *p*" were reporting a contentful experience, then it could certainly look *to a subject S* as if *X*, even if it were perfectly plain that *X* were not so—for instance, if *S* were hallucinating an airport lounge while standing alone on an empty beach.

37. Byrne (2009) argues that some uses of "looks *F*" do reflect contents of experience, but grants Travis's semantic objection and goes on to argue for the Content View on the grounds that it offers the best explanation of perceptual illusion.

assessable for accuracy. Rebutting this objection thus contributes to defending the claim that the best explanation for our classifications is that experiences themselves can be accurate or inaccurate.

What structure would the phenomenal character of a visual perceptual experience have to have, in order for the psychological objection to hold? There seem to be two answers:

Answer 1: Visual phenomenology is a pure raw feel or Reidian sensation.

Answer 2: When a visual experience is not hallucinatory, its visual phenomenology does not consist, even in part, in the subject's perceiving properties.

According to Answer 2, in non-hallucinatory experiences, we perceive entities that are concrete and worldly. If the entities are objects and we perceive both the objects and some of their properties, then this will allow us to define a sense of *looks F* that picks out the properties objects look to us to have. This sense could then figure in the Argument from Appearing, and in the descriptions of *Fishtank, Lunchtime*, and the other experiences we have discussed. So this model of visual experience does not support the psychological objection, which denies that any special use of *looks* could be defined that would exclusively track what's presented in visual phenomenology. To support the psychological objection, it has to be the case that properties are never presented in visual phenomenology. Travis seems to endorse this conclusion. He writes:

Perception can . . . make the world bear on what one is to think by furnishing access to things being as they are. Insofar as things being as they are is a different candidate object of perception than *A* being *F, G, H, . . .* then that's a reason not to think that perception or its phenomenal character (whatever that is) involves a commitment to the truth of some proposition. (p. 20, unpublished, quoted with permission)

According to Travis, non-hallucinatory experiences are perceptual relations to "things being as they are," and things being as they are differs from objects (or anything) having properties, and from anything individuated by objects and the properties they instantiate. The phenomenal character of non-hallucinatory experiences consists in this relation. Travis's position is a version of what we can call Radical Naïve Realism. According to Radical Naïve Realism, all non-hallucinatory experiences consist in a perceptual relation to something other than properties.

> **Radical Naïve Realism**: All non-hallucinatory experiences consist in a perceptual relation to a worldly item, and properties are not among the things the subject is perceptually related to.

A form of Radical Naïve Realism is the Pure Object View, according to which non-hallucinatory experiences are perceptual relations to objects.

> **Pure Object View**: All non-hallucinatory experiences are perceptual relations to objects and only to objects.[38]

A potential proponent of the Pure Object View is Bill Brewer, who writes:

> The only alternative to characterizing experience by its representational content is to characterize it as a direct presentation to the subject of certain objects which constitute the way things are for him in enjoying that perceptual experience. Call these the direct objects of experiences: the objects which constitute the subjective character of perceptual experience.[39]

Brewer holds that in cases of illusion, "direct objects" of experience "have the power to mislead us, in virtue of their perceptually

---

38. The Pure Object View could be extended to non-hallucinatory experiences generally, including illusions. If extended in this way, it would become a version of Naïve Realism on which the main division among experiences is between hallucination on the one hand, and non-hallucinatory experiences on the other. (Byrne and Logue [2008] call this VI versus H disjunctivism.)

39. Brewer (2006), 168.

relevant similarities with other things" (2006, 168). Since similarities have to hold in virtue of something, it seems that they would
hold in virtue of properties of the objects. And at that point it is
hard to see how the resulting version of Naïve Realism avoids
perceived properties.[40]

Both Answer 1 (the raw-feel view) and Answer 2 (Radical
Naïve Realism) deny that properties ever figure in experiences.
(Answer 1 says the same about objects.) Phenomenologically this
is highly dubious, for reasons related to those that arose in defending premise (i) of the Argument from Appearing. Normally, when
we see objects, we can discern where they are in relation to us,
which bits of space they occupy, and in this informational feat
visual phenomenology does not seem to be merely incidental.
Visual phenomenology changes with big changes in what perception furnishes us access to. If we see a teapot in one case and a
writhing snake in another, then the specific conscious character of
each experience differs, as do the features of the world to which
the experience gives us access. Within a Naïve Realist framework,
we need properties (or something in the vicinity, such as centering
features or tropes) to specify which aspects of the experience we
pick up on in experience, and correlatively which specific phenomenal character an experience has. Radical Naïve Realism
denies, implausibly, that experience presents us with properties of
the things we see.

Radical Naïve Realism is radical in another way as well. It
denies the intuition that something is missing from cases of predicative veridical illusion, such as the case of Simone (2.1). Since
according to Radical Naïve Realism, we never perceive properties
(or property-instances) of the things we see, there is nothing short
of completely successful perceptual contact when blue things
look blue to Simone due to an intervention that removes a color

---

40. Ultimately, Brewer's theory of illusions assimilates them to
strongly veridical experiences, with the only errors in the picture located
downstream of experiences.

illusion to which she would otherwise be subject if left to her own devices. Radical Naïve Realism denies that there are any super-strongly veridical experiences. In contrast, standard Naïve Realism may take superstrongly veridical experiences to be the central case of visual perceptual experience from which theorizing should proceed.

Does standard Naïve Realism provide any support for the psychological objection? In standard formulations of Naïve Realism, the worldly items that partly constitute the relevant class of non-hallucinatory experiences are individuated by both objects and properties. Since different proponents of Naïve Realism define this class differently, we can call such experiences Good, and say that Naïve Realists differ amongst themselves about which non-hallucinatory experiences are Good. But standardly, Naïve Realists take Good experiences to be relations to both objects and properties.[41] And to the extent that Good experiences are tied closely to knowledge, they will be superstrongly veridical.[42] For instance, John Campbell writes:

41. Martin talks about experiences as relations to events involving properties, rather than objects having properties; e.g., the ball's hitting the cube, rather than the fact that the ball is hitting the cube. A more fine-grained ontology than I will assume here would recognize metaphysical distinctions between the ball hitting the cube, the ball's hitting the cube, and the fact that the ball is hitting the cube, considering the first two events rather than facts. For the purpose of understanding the relationship between Naïve Realism and the Content View, it won't matter if we ignore the ontological differences between these relata, since they are all individuated at least partly by perceived objects and properties (the ball, the cube, being hit, being in the process of being hit, etc.). Depending on how the perceived properties are construed, Naïve Realism also comes in a trope version and a universal version.

42. Arguably, in the case of Simone, the connection between the belief that the cube is green, the experience in which it looks green, and the cube's being green is too spotty to support knowledge. In nearby worlds where there is no intervention to cancel out Simone's illusion, her experience would lead her to make a mistake about the cube's color.

On a Relational View, the phenomenal character of your experience, as you look around the room, is constituted by the actual
layout of the room itself: which particular objects are there,
their intrinsic properties, such as colour and shape, and how
they are arranged in relation to one another and to you. (2002,
116)

Likewise, M. G. F. Martin describes Good experiences by invoking
both objects and properties: "The Naïve Realist claims that . . .
some of the objects of perception—the concrete individuals, their
properties, and the events these partake in—are constituents of
the experience" (2005, 39).

A similar commitment is incurred by Kennedy and by Mark
Johnston.[43] To oppose the Content View, these proponents of
Naïve Realism need grounds for denying that token Good experiences are accurate with respect to the situation in which they are
had. It is hard to see what grounds these might be. According to
one line of thought, Good experiences (as standard Naïve Realism
construes them) are not accurate, because it is not possible for
such experiences to be inaccurate. This line of thought assumes
that it makes sense to ascribe accuracy to a state, only if it is
possible for instances of that state to be inaccurate. The assumption, however, is wrong. The state of believing that 3+5=8 is never
inaccurate. But it doesn't follow that the belief is not true.[44]

43. Kennedy (2009): "Naïve Realists think of veridical experience as a
relation between subjects and material particulars and their perceptible
properties." Johnston (2006) discusses superstrongly veridical experiences explicitly (though not under that label) and argues that they are not
fundamentally contentful states, but rather states of perceptual awareness.
44. Of course, experiences as standard Naïve Realism construes them
differ structurally from beliefs. The present point is just that it is not in
general true that a state is assessable for accuracy only if it is possible for
instances of that state to be false. This is shown by the case of beliefs
whose contents are necessarily true propositions. So, no such general
point supports the claim that strongly veridical experiences as Naïve Realism construes them are assessable for accuracy.

According to a different attempt to deny that Good experiences (as standard Naïve Realism construes them) are accurate, if a state is accurate, then it must be possible to compare the state with the situation of which it is accurate. As standard versions of Naïve Realism construe Good experiences, those experiences contain the relevant situations as constituents. One might conclude from this that no comparison is possible. But there is no metaphysical bar to comparing a state that is partly composed of a situation with the situation of which it is partly composed. (Compare: when a Russellian proposition composed of an object and a property is evaluated with respect to worlds where the object exists, a proposition that is partly composed of an object is compared with a situation containing that very object.) The relata are different, even if overlapping.

If the idea of comparison still seems strained, the feeling of strain seems rooted in the redundancy of the perceived situation, which figures on both sides of the comparison. If the state in the alleged comparison is a state of seeing Franco's sitting down, then in describing the state, we have already described the situation in which the state is had: it is a situation in which Franco is sitting down. Since a situation is not accurate with respect to itself, it may seem as if any comparison covertly targets an aspect of the state that is separable from the things and properties perceived. Since Naïve Realism denies precisely that there are any such separable aspects, such comparison would be illicit.

In response, the Naïve Realist is committed to the idea that perceptual contact with Franco and some of his properties constitutes the subjective character of the experience. When we focus on the subjective character of the experience, comparing it with the situation in which it is had seems to make sense, no matter what metaphysical structure it may have. Franco appears to be sitting down, and we can ask whether things are as they appear. In making this comparison, we don't have to make any assumptions about the underlying metaphysical structure of the experience. So the idea of comparing a Good experience with the situation in which it is had is not illicit, even if those experiences are structured the way Naïve Realism says they are.

In summary, nothing in the structure of Good experiences as standard Naïve Realism construes them precludes experiences from presenting it as being the case that the object seen has the properties seen, and nothing prevents such experiences from having a presentational character. The contrast drawn earlier between experiences and hopes holds independently of whether Naïve Realism is true. If so, it is hard to see the daylight between standard Naïve Realism and the claim that Good experiences are accurate.

2.6. THE SIGNIFICANCE OF THE CONTENT VIEW

We have seen that the Content View can be resisted by denying that properties are presented in experience. We can also ask: is the Content View unavoidable, so long as properties are presented in experience? If so, this would be a powerful philosophical result. There are many ways in which properties could be presented in experience. In particular, properties are presented in experience, even according to theories that are traditionally taken to be at odds with the idea that experiences have contents, such as Naïve Realism as it is standardly construed. If the Content View is unavoidable given widely accepted assumptions, then it will not be a parochial thesis, of interest only in a small corner of philosophy, but will rather be a thesis that can be used in the analysis of perception across a wide range of theoretical assumptions. Just as important questions about belief are usefully posed within a framework assuming that beliefs have accuracy conditions, the same may be true of perception.

One way for properties to be presented in experience leads directly to the Content View. Call this way the Property View.

> **Property View**: All experiences involve relations to properties presented in experience, and are accurate only if those properties are instantiated.[45]

Since the Property View says that experiences have accuracy conditions that derive from the properties presented in experience, it leads to the Content View (given the assumption defended earlier that these properties are conveyed to the subject). Since the Property View entails the Content View, to oppose the Content View, one must also oppose the Property View.

The Property View may be resisted in several ways. First, properties might figure in experience in a way that avoids it. For instance, according to classical sense-datum theories of the sort defended by Russell (1912), experiences consist in perceptions of sense-data (construed as mental objects) and their properties. The properties had by sense-data were thought to be different from properties of external objects, but systematically related to them. For instance, whereas apples are red, the sense-data you have when seeing an apple are red' (red-prime). And since sense-data were thought to be located in mental space (rather than in the same space as the external apple), they couldn't have exactly the same spatial properties (notably depth) as the external objects that were thought to cause them.[46] The discrepancy between the properties of external objects and the properties of sense-data makes the latter ill-suited to figure in accuracy conditions, and so is at odds with the second conjunct of the Property View. If an experience as the sense-datum theory construes it is allowed to count as accurate, it won't have this status thanks to the "primed" properties of sense-data, it will have this status thanks to the properties of external objects. So some versions of the classical

45. "Property" can be construed broadly to include either universals or tropes or centering features, as none of these options alters the dialectic surrounding the Argument from Appearing.

46. For discussion of depth and other spatial properties, see Foster (2000).

sense-datum theory that avoid the Property View can nonetheless embrace the Content View.[47] Second, Reidian sensations or raw feels involve properties to the extent that they purport to provide qualitative types of experience (so that two perceivers, or the same perceiver in different situations, could have experiences with the same raw feel). Since these properties are not presented in experience as properties instantiated by anything at all, the Property View is avoided.

The pure raw feel view and the classical sense-datum theory each face substantial objections. First, according to the raw feel view, neither objects nor properties are presented in experience, which leaves it mysterious what role experience plays in enabling the subject to distinguish objects from one another and figure from ground. Second, the raw feel view allows that two experiences could be phenomenally the same, while varying enormously in which contents it would be natural to believe on the basis of the experience. Finally, the classical sense-datum theory faces the challenge of making sense of the notion of mental space to house sense-data, where mental space is distinct from the space in which our bodies and other external bodies are found. A full case against each of these views would require separate discussion, but these objections suggest that neither position provides a powerful basis from which to deny the Property View.

Many proponents of Naïve Realism, including Campbell, Brewer, Martin, and Mark Johnston, have been vocal critics of the Content View. As we've seen, standard Naïve Realism is

---

47. For instance, nothing in Russell's theory rules out that an experience of seeing an (external) apple is accurate, even on the assumption that the experience consists in the perception of sense-data. One could consistently hold that such an experience is accurate if it is caused by something that has properties systematically related to the "primed" properties of the sense-data. And primed properties could be presented in experience in our sense, since sense-data are not experiences all by themselves—the subject has to be related to them via a mental act.

hard-pressed to avoid the Property View. The most stable way for Naïve Realists to oppose the Content View is by embracing the Pure Object View, or some other form of Radical Naïve Realism. But Radical Naïve Realism runs afoul of phenomenological considerations. If standard Naïve Realism can't avoid the Property View, it must embrace the Content View as well.

Naïve Realism and the Strong Content View

When proponents of Naïve Realism criticize the idea that experiences have contents, their criticism is best understood as directed at a strong form of the Content View according to which experiences are fundamentally structured as a propositional attitude. One version of this idea is the Strong Content View:

> **Strong Content View**: All visual perceptual experiences consist fundamentally in the subject's bearing a propositional attitude toward the contents of her experience.

The Strong Content View is not entailed by either the Content View or the Property View. It is compatible with both the Property View and the Content View that experiences (or some subset of them) are fundamentally structured by a perceptual relation, either to external objects (as in Naïve Realism) or to mental objects (as in the classical sense-datum theory). So neither the Content View nor the Property View is committed to the Strong Content View.

Given this difference between the structures posited by Naïve Realism and the Strong Content View, one might think that these views are incompatible. But this claim is an overgeneralization, and the difference in the structures per se is of little philosophical interest. We can see this by considering versions of these views that are clearly at odds, and contrasting them with versions of the views that have close affinities.

Versions of the Strong Content View according to which no contents are individuated by perceived objects are clearly at odds with Naïve Realism. And some versions of Naïve Realism are clearly incompatible with the Strong Content View. These include standard Naïve Realism, Radical Naïve Realism, and "negative" disjunctivism, according to which hallucinations consist entirely in a negative epistemic fact, rather than in a mental state with a specific structure.[48]

Other versions of each view, however, bring them closer together. For instance, as McDowell (1996) construes facts, facts are both true propositions, and are also concrete things that can be perceived.[49] There could be a version of standard Naïve Realism that took facts so construed to be constituents of super-strongly veridical experiences. This version of Naïve Realism would clearly be compatible with the Strong Content View.

There are also versions of the Strong Content View that closely resemble standard Naïve Realism. First, according to content disjunctivism, the contents of non-hallucinatory experiences (such as the strongly veridical *Lunchtime*, or the illusory *Fishtank*) are individuated by objects that are seen (e.g., the sandwich, the fish, etc), whereas the contents of hallucinations that are indiscriminable from these experiences—such as a hallucination of a sandwich that looks just like your lunch, or of a fishtank—would have contents that are not individuated by any perceived objects.[50] It is also possible to formulate content disjunctivism in a way that individuates the contents of strongly veridical experiences by perceived properties, as well as by perceived objects.

The structure of such experiences still differs from the structure posited by Naïve Realism, on the assumption (contra McDowell) that propositions are never also worldly items that can be perceived. But a necessary (and possibly sufficient) condition for

48. The epistemic conception of hallucination was first explained and defended by Martin (2004). See also Martin (2006). Pautz (2010) discusses the distinction between negative and positive disjunctivism.

49. McDowell (1996).

50. For defenses of content disjunctivism, see Bach (ms.), Byrne and Logue (2008), Schellenberg (2011), and Tye (2007).

entertaining the relevant sort of proposition is to perceive an object and a cluster of its properties. It may seem merely a matter of terminology whether the experience is the entertaining of the object- and property-involving proposition, as per this kind of content disjunctivist, or whether the experience is the perception of objects and properties that gives rise to the entertaining of such a proposition. Whether or not this issue is merely terminological, this sort of content disjunctivism remains closely related to standard Naïve Realism.

Second, there could be a disjunctivist version of the Strong Content View according to which strongly veridical experiences are a variety of factive propositional attitude (such as seeing that p), while other experiences are non-factive propositional attitudes.

In the end, whatever dialectical status Naïve Realism has in relation to the Strong Content View, it seems clear that Naïve Realism and the Content View are compatible. Even the forms of standard Naïve Realism that are incompatible with the Strong Content View are compatible with the Content View. To reject the Content View while maintaining Naïve Realism, it is necessary to move away from standard Naïve Realism and toward the radical form, which I have argued is implausible.

It is easy to get the impression from recent discussions that fundamentally different approaches to perception are exemplified by Naïve Realism on the one hand and the Content View on the other.[51] While the impression of a great divide between these positions is sociologically apt, philosophically it is overdrawn, and it makes a poor guide to the underlying issues. The philosophical divide is not between these approaches per se, but between positions on two questions. The first question concerns whether properties are presented in experience. The Content View stands or falls with the answer to this question. If experiences do not present us with properties (as per Radical Naïve

51. E.g., Campbell (2002, chap. 6), Martin (2002), Pautz (2010), Schellenberg (2011), and Logue (2011).

Realism and the raw feel view), then the Content View is false. The second question concerns whether there is any need to individuate experiences by the particular things that the subject of the experience perceives. Naïve Realism stands or falls with the answer to this question. If experiences are not individuated by such objects, then Naïve Realism is false. To the extent that these two questions are independent of each other, Naïve Realism and the Content View are independent of each other, too.

Chapter 3

How Can We Discover the Contents of Experience?

I'VE ARGUED THAT VISUAL PERCEPTUAL EXPERIENCES HAVE CONTENTS. But which contents do they have?

The question has two aspects. First, there are a number of abstract objects that contents could be, corresponding to different kinds of propositions, and we can ask which such abstract objects are best for characterizing the contents of experience. Second, no matter which such abstract objects turn out to be best for this, we can also ask which properties things look to have when we see them. Let us examine each of these aspects in a bit more detail.

Propositions themselves can be structured or unstructured, and there are different ways of being structured. For instance, purely Russellian propositions have a structure akin to syntax, and their elements are objects and properties. Alternatively, Fregean propositions are structured by a concatenation of modes of presentation of objects and properties. Unstructured propositions are sets of possible worlds, or sets of centered worlds. And there are variants of these proposals as well. When we ask which contents experiences have, part of what we're asking is which abstract objects best characterize how things look to us when we have visual experiences. So what's most important to consider when comparing proposals about different kinds of propositions is what sort of facts about accuracy conditions and phenomenal character each kind of abstract object could be invoked to explain.

No matter which kinds of abstract objects turn out to be best for characterizing experiences, properties will figure in these contents in one way or another: as properties had by things in the possible (centered) worlds that constitute an unstructured proposition, as constituents of a structured Russellian proposition itself, or as referents of modes of presentation that constitute a Fregean proposition. I will say that a property is represented in experience if it figures in experience contents in any of these ways. So, if a property is *presented* in experience in any of the ways discussed in the Argument from Appearing, then I will say it is *represented* in experience. I will also say that a property is represented in experience if it figures in experience as a condition on reference imposed by Fregean modes of presentation.[1]

The second aspect of our question concerns which properties experiences can represent. Here is where the Rich Content View enters the picture. When you see a bowl of fruit, you can (usually) recognize the kinds of fruit in the bowl. But is it part of your visual experience that the bowl contains fruit (pineapple, banana, grapes, and so on)? Or do you just visually experience colors and shapes, and then go on to judge that there is fruit in the bowl? Once the Content View is on the table, we can formulate the question about which properties are represented in experience, without first settling what kinds of abstract objects are best to use in characterizing the contents of experience.

In this chapter I will discuss how one might reasonably proceed to discover which properties experiences represent. Several natural starting points suggest themselves. First, one might reasonably ask what role, if any, introspection can play. Second, over recent years, philosophers such as Fred Dretske, Jerry Fodor, Ruth Millikan, David Papineau, and others have developed a variety of naturalistic theories that aim to account for what makes it the case that we have contentful mental states, and (in the case of some of these theories) what makes it the case that these states have the contents they do. Some of these philosophers, and others, such as Robert Stalnaker and Michael Tye,

1. They don't figure in this way in the two-dimensionalist Fregean views we considered, but there could be a Fregean view in which they did.

explicitly apply such theories to the case of perceptual experiences. It would be natural to ask whether these applications shed any light on the question of which properties visual experiences represent.

I will argue that neither introspection alone nor the naturalistic theories just mentioned enable us to discover the contents of experiences, and so a different method is needed. I think such a method is available: the method of phenomenal contrast. This chapter aims to make explicit what that method is and to defend it. It is thus addressed to skeptics who doubt that there is any tractable way to discover which properties experiences can represent, and to non-skeptics who would like to know which properties these are.

3.1 INTROSPECTION

Suppose you are looking at a bowl of expertly designed wax fruit. You have a visual experience when you see this scene, and we can ask which properties your experience represents as being instantiated in the scene before you. Here are two hypotheses. According to the color-shape hypothesis, your visual experience represents the colors and shapes of the wax fruit but does not go so far as to represent that it is fruit. Moreover, the wax fruit actually has the colors and shapes that the experience represents them as having. If the color-shape hypothesis about the contents of experience is correct, then the experience is veridical, because it does not attribute to the wax fruits any properties that they lack. You may go on to form a false belief to the effect that there are cherries in the bowl, but if you do that, your error will remain at the level of belief and will not infect your experience, since your experience is not committal on whether the colored shapes in the bowl are cherries or not. In contrast, according to the cherry-content hypothesis, your visual experience represents the property of being a cherry, and its contents include that there are cherries in the bowl.

Could you decide between these hypotheses just by introspectively reflecting on your experience? It seems plain that in seeing the fruit bowl (or even in merely hallucinating), one can know by introspection that one is not having an experience as of a busy airport or of an undifferentiated expanse of blue. Introspection can rule out many proposed contents as inadequate to the phenomenal character of the experience and thus is not completely useless as a means of discovering which contents an experience has. It can take us part of the way. But it does not take us far enough. If introspection could tell us whether the color-shape hypothesis or the cherry-content hypothesis were correct, then we would not expect to find disagreement about these hypotheses in the first place: the same hypothesis would seem obvious to everyone. But that is not what we find. To some people, neither hypothesis is obviously correct; to others, hypotheses favoring the Rich Content View are obviously correct; and to others still, such hypotheses are obviously incorrect.[2]

It may seem strange that introspection cannot decide between these two hypotheses, since the contents of experience are supposed to reflect the phenomenal character of the experience. Moreover, states with phenomenal character may seem to be intrinsically

2. For example, in his influential discussion of various uses of "looks," Jackson (1977) defines the phenomenal sense in such a way that it picks out only non-K properties, suggesting that these are the only properties that would be needed to characterize visual phenomenal states. In contrast, Hyslop (1983) seems to find the Rich Content View obvious: "Objects seen in circumstances where they are distinguishably themselves are not seen as a congeries of shape and colour. The way an elephant looks at, say, 10 yards is not exhausted by delineations of shape and colour. Indeed, it takes both effort and training to limit oneself to such facts. An elephant at 10 yards has the elephant look, looks elephantly" (535).

the sort of states that are accessible to introspection.[3] But even if we grant that phenomenal character is intrinsically accessible to introspection, it does not follow that introspection tells us sufficiently precisely which contents such states have. Part of what makes it difficult to generate such a precise output of introspection is that it is not clear exactly what procedure a person would follow if she wanted to use introspection to ascertain which contents her experience had. This difficulty comes in a practical and in a theoretical version. The practical version is relatively innocuous: it is unclear what would count as following an instruction to introspectively reflect on one's visual experience. Stare into space and see what comes to mind? Focus on features of the objects around you? Imagine how you'd describe your experience to someone who wanted to know? Although this unclarity may prevent an individual from easily assessing whether introspection alone can reveal what contents experiences have, it doesn't by itself refute the proposal that introspection is indeed capable of discovering this. Merely having practical difficulty discerning what kind of reflection is introspective reflection is compatible with there being such a thing as distinctively introspective reflection, and with that kind of reflection informing us of what contents experiences have.

The theoretical version of the difficulty, in contrast, poses a problem for relying exclusively on introspection to decide between competing hypotheses about the contents of experience—or relying on it to decide from scratch, without initial

3. This issue is at the center of the controversy over whether there can be phenomenal consciousness without what Ned Block calls "access-consciousness." See Block (2002, 2008). However this issue is settled, it would stretch the notion of the phenomenal too far if there were phenomenally conscious states that were necessarily completely under the first-person radar. Whether this amounts to denying Block's claim that there can be what he calls phenomenal consciousness without access consciousness depends on what the first-personal radar is and what notion of access is relevant to access consciousness.

hypotheses, which contents these are. The theoretical difficulty concerns what kind of procedure or faculty introspection is. On a domain-general model, introspection allows one to discover the current occupants of one's stream of consciousness, whatever they are; but it may not be introspectively obvious if an occupant is a visual experience, as opposed to a different kind of mental state or event.[4] If this model best reflects the nature of introspection, then even while introspecting correctly, one could unknowingly introspectively attend to something other than visual experience. Given this possibility, verdicts delivered by introspection that purport to be verdicts on the contents of visual experience may in fact be about the contents of some other kind of state, such as a judgment. These considerations are general, suggesting that the same limitations apply when using introspection to learn about any mental states, not just visual experiences.

If the domain-general model of introspection were not apt, this problem could not arise. An alternative model of introspection is a domain-specific model. On a domain-specific model, introspection of visual experience is a different kind of reflection (perhaps because it is a different kind of procedure) from introspection of other kinds of occupants of the stream of consciousness. If this kind of reflection goes as it should, it will result in beliefs about visual experience, rather than in beliefs about some other kind of occupant of the stream of consciousness.

It is doubtful that the domain-specific model is apt, if introspection is construed as a procedure whose employment is an optional addition to the experience itself. There doesn't seem to be any special sort of procedure that can be used to reflect on, say, olfactory

---

4. Neither the domain-general model nor the domain-specific model needs to rely on the idea that there is such a thing as a stream of consciousness with occupants. Either could be considered a procedure that purports to discern that one is currently in a mental state, without discerning exactly what kind of state it is.

experience, but cannot be used to reflect on visual experience. On the assumption that the procedure is a kind of attention, for example, there seems to be only one kind of attention at the personal level, which can be variously directed to what is seen or what is smelled. A piece of evidence for this is that directing attention in one of these ways can interfere with directing attention in the other.

The only way in which introspection could plausibly be domain-specific is if it were construed as a perspective on experience that was somehow built into visual experience.[5] Either such a perspective would often be inaccurate in its portrayal of the contents of experience (even when there were no intrinsic defects in the experience) or it would not. If it were often inaccurate, then it could not be used to settle which contents experiences have. If it were reliably accurate, then in principle it would indeed be able to settle such disputes. But the fact of disagreement calls into question whether we have any direct line of access from this perspective to what we report when we reflect on our experiences. Either way, then, introspection on its own, construed as a perspective on how things look that is built into our experiences, does not enable us to discover the contents of those experiences.

In the next section, I consider whether some influential naturalistic theories of content for mental states might be employed to decide which contents experiences have.

3.2 NATURALISTIC THEORIES OF CONTENT

According to some philosophers, for a mental state to have content is for it to represent that such-and-such conditions obtain,

5. Martin (2006) gestures toward the idea that introspection is a perspective on experience that is built into it.

where representation is a kind of causal covariation with those conditions. I will argue that even if such theories are true, they will not help us discover the contents of experience.

Michael Tye has developed a causal-covariation theory for visual experiences.[6] He states the theory as follows:

> For each state S of object x, within the relevant set of alternative states of x:
> S represents that P = If optimal conditions obtain, S would be tokened in x if and only if and because P.[7]

Robert Stalnaker (2003) endorses something close to this theory as well.

One might think that the causal-covariation theory would-make straightforward predictions about which contents experiences have, by licensing the following procedure: pick an experience, identify the optimal conditions for having it, and find out what causes and covaries with the experience under those conditions. Call this the *experience-first procedure*. If the causal-covariation theory is true, then—one might think—the content of the experience would be the proposition that such-and-such obtains, where such-and-such is what causes and covaries with the state. We would then either have to take these predictions as the truth about what the contents of experiences are, or else refute the theory.

To follow the experience-first procedure, one would have to identify which experiences in counterfactual circumstances (namely, other optimal conditions) are the same as the one we were asking about. This is not something the causal-covariation

---

6. Tye (1995) calls these "simple perceptual sensations," which are supposed to be outputs of what he calls "specialized sensory modules" (103). Tye's use of "sensation" differs from Reid's, which was mentioned in chapter 1.

7. Tye (1995, 101). As we will see, this is only part of the theory. A separate part tells us what makes such a state an experience.

theory itself tells us.[8] We would need a way to identify which experiences across possible worlds are the same, holding constant the essential features of the experiences, whatever they are, while allowing others to vary. Without a way to do this, we would not be able to assess whether the experience whose contents we are asking about *would be tokened* in x. If we can't assess that, then we can't consider what situations would cause and covary with such counterfactual tokenings.

Until we have settled what contents the experience has, however, it is difficult to reidentify experiences across worlds. It might be plausible to suppose that if my current experience has the content p, then any experience in some other possible world that's identical to it will also have that content—but which contents my experience has is what we're trying to find out. Moreover, our initial uncertainty about which contents experiences have is also uncertainty about their exact phenomenal character. The phenomenal character is no more accessible to introspection than are the contents of experience. We are thus also precluded from using the phenomenal character to reidentify experiences.

There is a different potential procedure for discovery, however, that does not face this difficulty. Instead of beginning with an experience and trying to identify it across possible worlds, the alternative procedure begins with some other state—as it might be, a neural state, or a functional state of some sort—initially ignoring the question of whether this state has the status of an experience (or indeed of any mental representation). Call this the

8. It need not be a fault of the causal covariation theory that it is silent on how any mental states it applies to are identified across worlds. The causal covariation theory was developed in an effort to show that mental states could represent happenings in the world, consistently with physicalism. If the theory is correct, then it seems to succeed in doing that, even if it does not tell us how to identify experiences across worlds. Even if for some reason the theory turned out not to be consistent with physicalism, it could still be correct in holding that mental states represent what they causally covary with under optimal conditions.

information-state-first procedure. The next step is to try to find out
what conditions are optimal for being in this state, and what
causes and covaries with the state under those conditions. Finally,
with the informational content of the state in hand, one consults
the theory's criterion for being an experience, as opposed to being
merely a subpersonal state or a mental state of some other sort.
For Tye, such a state is an experience if at least some of its contents
have the proper functional role in fixing belief; Stalnaker makes a
similar, albeit more tentative, suggestion.[9] The contents of the
informational state that plays the functional role associated with
experience would then be the contents of an experience.

The limits of this method become apparent when we consider
the relationship between the experience and the neural state.
Either the neural state underlies the experience in the manner of a
realizer (let's consider being identical to it to be a special case of
this), or it is only part of the realizer of the experience. Only in the
first case will we have learned what contents the experience has
from learning what contents the neural state has. For the method
to be useable and informative in such cases, our epistemic position
at the start has to be this: we have good reason to think that the
neural state is the complete realizer of the experience, but we don't
know what contents the experience has. Since we don't now have
much understanding of what sorts of neural states exhaustively
realize experiences, we can't actually use this method—even if the
causal-covariation theory is true.

Now suppose the informational state (neural state, or functional state) is only a partial realizer of the experience. Then, if we
apply this method, by the lights of the causal covariation theory,
we will have learned (using causal-covariation theory) something
about what contents the experience includes. This would be a partial discovery about the contents of experience. We won't, however, have put any upper limits on which contents these can be,
and so applying the method in this sort of case may not always

9. Stalnaker (2003, 103), Tye (1995, chap. 5).

help us decide between the hypotheses of the sort discussed at the start, and in particular it may not help us decide whether the Rich Content View is true.

Finally, even if some application of the method derived from the causal-covariation theory can tell us about the contents of an experience, it does not let us start with the experiences we want to know about, such as the experience of seeing faces, or experiences whose contents are at issue in controversies over whether they represent kind properties, and whether they represent causal properties.[10] Instead, we have to happen upon any experiences whose contents we want to know about indirectly, by starting with an informational state.

The method derived from the causal covariation theory thus has its limits, given our epistemic situation. I will now argue that another method is available that can produce better results.

3.3 THE METHOD OF PHENOMENAL CONTRAST

The method of phenomenal contrast is a kind of reasoning about special pairs of overall experiences. It will therefore be useful to reclaim the word *experience* as a label for overall experiences. "Experience" is no longer an abbreviation for visual perceptual experiences.

The method of phenomenal contrast is a way to test hypotheses about the contents of visual experience. Its main strategy is to

---

10. The experience of seeing faces is important in understanding the nature of certain pathologies of belief, such as Capgras syndrome, in which subjects believe that their spouse has been replaced by an impostor. Discussion of the nature of this syndrome focuses on whether subjects are responding (normally or abnormally) to a normal experience, or to an abnormal one. To settle this, we need to know which properties experiences of faces normally represent. Controversies over the representation of kind and causal properties in experience are discussed in part II.

find something that the target hypothesis purports to explain, and then see whether it provides the best explanation of that phenomenon. Instead of taking a specific visual experience as input and delivering a verdict on its contents as output, the method's starting point is a target hypothesis, and it aims to reach a yes-or-no verdict on that hypothesis. It is thus a way of testing hypotheses, rather than a way of generating hypotheses in the first place.

Since contents of visual experiences are non-arbitrarily related to their phenomenal character, any target hypothesis will predict that certain pairs of such experiences that differ with respect to the hypothesized contents will differ phenomenally as well. It is thus possible to use the phenomenal contrast as the thing to be explained. The target explanation will say the two overall experiences contrast phenomenally because one of them includes a visual experience that has the hypothesized contents, while the other one includes a visual experience that does not have the hypothesized contents.[11]

Several debates about perception can be construed as employing the method of phenomenal contrast. Consider the supervenience thesis (often labeled "intentionalism"), which states that any two perceptual experiences with the same representational properties have the same phenomenal character. Some philosophers argue that cases of size and color constancy show intentionalism to be false. In response, intentionalists try to find differences in representational properties accompanying the phenomenal contrast. Peacocke (1983) discussed a case of seeing two trees of the same size on a straight street. He claimed that we don't suffer

11. If the target hypothesis does not figure in the best explanation of the phenomenal contrast then, when applied properly, the method will reveal this. But it will not necessarily identify which explanation of the phenomenal contrast is the best. (The target hypothesis might turn out to be worse than all the alternatives.) So although the method is a version of inference to the best explanation, it is not a version that always yields a verdict as to which explanation is the best.

any illusion about whether the trees are the same size (they look to be the same size), and yet there is a sense in which the tree that is farther away looks smaller than the tree that is closer. Much debate ensued about how best to account for the phenomenal contrast between the two trees—whether it was a difference in content, and if so, how the content of the experience of seeing each tree differed. Here is an example of a phenomenal contrast serving as an explanandum that hypotheses about the content of experience compete to explain.

The same argumentative role is played by phenomenal difference between visual experiences of spectrally inverted perceivers. Such perceivers allegedly have phenomenally different visual experiences (one is phenomenally like a normal experience of seeing unpeeled cucumbers and the other is phenomenally like a normal experience of seeing ripe strawberries) yet stand in the same kind of causal relation to the physical property identified (for the sake of the thought-experiment) with redness.[12] Subsequent debate has revolved around whether the phenomenal difference is a difference in content, and, if so, what contents each visual experience has.

Both of these debates involve phenomenal contrasts that various positions compete in trying to explain. The phenomenal contrasts involved in perceptual constancy and in putative spectral inversion pose long-standing challenges to psychology and philosophy, and therefore are already salient.[13] But the method of phenomenal contrast can also be used to test hypotheses that single out a specific property, such as the hypothesis that causal relations can be represented in visual experience, or the hypothesis that when you see the fruit bowl, your visual experience represents that there are grapes in the bowl. These hypotheses are

12. For discussion of intentionalism and the inverted spectrum, see the Introduction in Byrne and Hilbert (1997) and the papers therein.

13. On spectral inversion, see Locke (1689/1975) and Nida-Rumelin (1996). On constancy, see Russell (1997/1912) and Smith (2002).

more specific than intentionalism. When the method is employed to test them, a pair of contrasting overall experiences has to be sought. The contrasts that figure in the applications of this method are not likely to already be subjects of debate. Applying the method requires some creativity.

An Illustration

We can illustrate how the method works by considering the hypothesis that visual experiences can represent the property of being caused by something. (This example is discussed in more detail in chapter 5.) Let this be the target hypothesis in our example. Our target contents are contents involving causal properties. We then consider a pair of experiences with the following two features.

- First, one of the overall experiences in the pair is a reasonable candidate for including a visual experience that represents causation (the target property). This will be the *target experience*. An example for the case of causation might be an overall experience in which one flicks a light switch and sees the light go on. This experience is a candidate for one that includes a visual experience that represents that the flicking of the switch caused the light to go on. In contrast, the other experience should clearly and uncontroversially include a visual experience that does *not* represent the target property (causation). This will be the *contrasting experience*. Here one might consider a similar sequence in which the light that turns on is at a great distance from the switch that is flicked.
- Second, the two overall experiences in the pair (the target experience and the contrasting experience) fairly obviously differ phenomenally; consequently, people who may ultimately disagree about the target hypothesis would nonetheless agree that the two experiences exhibit a phenomenal contrast.

If the target hypothesis best explains the contrast, then it will be true of the visual experience in the target experience but not true of the visual experience in the contrasting experience. According to this explanation, the reason there is a phenomenal contrast between the experiences is that one includes a visual experience that represents the target property while the other includes a visual experience that does not represent the target property.

The method of phenomenal contrast thus starts off with an intuition that two overall experiences in a pair contrast phenomenally. Whether this first step can be plausibly challenged depends, naturally, on the examples one chooses. Some examples will be more powerful than others. But the kind of intuition on which the contrast method rests is simple and modest. Such intuitions concern whether there is a change in phenomenology between two sorts of situations. It would be quite radical to deny that there were *any* such cases in which introspection could detect a phenomenal contrast between overall experiences. In assuming that we have introspective access to such contrasts, we need not assume that such access alone can determine the exact contents of the visual parts of an overall experience.

This method can be seen as an attempt to split the difference between description and argument by starting with a minimal intuition and then mapping out exactly what an opponent of the target hypothesis would have to deny if she accepts the initial intuition. To use the method to decide whether the target hypothesis figures in the best explanation of the phenomenal contrast, the target explanation would have to be compared to alternative explanations. Which alternatives would have to be considered? Given the assumption that there is a phenomenal contrast, there will be three alternatives.

No difference in visual phenomenology

The phenomenal contrast is due exclusively to the presence of a phenomenally conscious non-sensory (e.g., cognitive) state in the target experience that is missing from the contrasting experience.

The idea that there are phenomenally conscious non-sensory states arises in discussion of "cognitive phenomenology."[14] A variety of theses grow out of this idea. When we apply the method of phenomenal contrast to test the Rich Content View, the only thesis in the area that is relevant is the relatively weak thesis.

Suppose you take a spoonful of soup. When you taste it, you find that it needs something, and wonder whether what it needs is salt.[15] Call this occasion of wondering w. Let us suppose that it is not possible to be in w without being in a phenomenal state. If so, then w is phenomenally conscious. But the status of w as phenomenally conscious allows that you could have been in w while being in a different phenomenal state from the one you were actually in. Compare the state of seeing Franco. Every time you're in that state, you're also in a visual phenomenal state of some sort. But it need not be the same phenomenal state each time. Franco looks different depending on whether he's sitting down, or dressed in orange, or riding his bicycle.

A relatively weak thesis about cognitive phenomenology is that there are episodes, such as wonderings, that are both non-sensory

14. For an overview, see Bayne and Montague, eds., *Cognitive Phenomenology* (Oxford University Press, 2011). Earlier work includes Strawson (1994), Siewert (1998), Horgan and Tienson (2002), and Pitt (2004). Sometimes the label "cognitive phenomenology" is used to exclude emotional states, bodily states, and background states that are phenomenally conscious. For us it won't be important exactly which non-perceptual, phenomenally conscious states are classified as cognitive. What will be more important is to understand a range of theses about paradigmatically cognitive states, such as occurrent thoughts of various kinds.

15. We can describe this occasion either as a state or an episode. The episode of wondering whether the soup needs salt is something that happens, necessarily, exactly when you wonder whether the soup needs salt. The state of wondering whether soup needs salt is a state you are in, necessarily, exactly when you wonder whether the soup needs salt. Since both the state and the episode necessarily co-occur, I'm going to ignore the distinction between them.

and phenomenally conscious. The weak thesis takes no stand on whether there is a phenomenal state that covaries with types of episodes, such as the type "wondering whether the soup needs salt."

Some philosophers accept the stronger claim that whenever you wonder whether the soup needs salt, you're in the same phenomenal state. And some have argued for an even stronger claim: that there is a unique phenomenal state that you're in when *and only when* you wonder whether the soup needs salt.[16] This stronger claim is an instance of what we can call the industrial-strength modal cognitive phenomenology thesis: for any occurrent non-sensory state-type M, there is some phenomenal state that covaries with M. (The thesis is only slightly longer than its name!)[17]

16. Philosophers who endorse both claims include Strawson (1994), Horgan and Tienson (2002), Siewert (2011), Pitt (2004), and Kriegel (2007).

17. Suppose the industrial-strength thesis is true, and there is some phenomenal state, call it Q, that covaries with the type of episode: wondering whether the soup needs salt. Saying this much tells us nothing about what kind of phenomenal state Q is. Q could belong to a qualitative type that is proprietarily cognitive; that is, one that has no constitutive connection to any of the senses. Or Q might be a special profile of visual, auditory, and bodily phenomenal states, such as a combination of a pain in the elbow, a tingle behind the neck, and a purple afterimage, and a complex state of acoustic imagery such as might accompany (or constitute) inner speech. (Compare the James-Lange theory of emotion [James 1884], one version of which identifies profiles of bodily sensations with specific emotions, yielding the prediction that getting into that specific bodily phenomenal state would suffice to get into the emotional state. The current claim we're discussing says something similar about occurrent thoughts—though the phenomenal state need not be limited to bodily states.) The industrial-strength thesis is silent on what qualitative type Q belongs to. The other theses mentioned in the text are also silent on the qualitative type of phenomenal states that may accompany occurrent thoughts.

When we apply the method of phenomenal contrast to test the
Rich Content View, we'll consider whether any non-sensory phenomenally conscious states explain the relevant phenomenal contrast. It won't matter whether any such states also satisfy the
stronger theses, such as the industrial-strength thesis.

No difference in the content of visual experience

The phenomenal contrast is due exclusively to the presence of a
nonrepresentational feature of the target experience that is missing
from the contrasting experience.

A nonrepresentational phenomenal property is a raw feel or
Reidian sensation. Raw feels may be appealed to in this type of
alternative in different ways. They may be said to belong to the
visual part of the target experience or not. (When they do, the
alternative grants that there is a phenomenal difference between
the visual parts of the target and the contrasting experiences
but denies that this visual phenomenal difference goes with any
difference in the contents of the visual experiences.) It may be
that a special raw feel is part of the target experience but not
part of the contrasting experience (or vice versa). Or it may be
that both experiences have raw feels, but they differ. Or it may
be that a special raw feel attaching to only one of the experiences combines with a non-phenomenal state to produce the
phenomenal contrast.

Non-targeted difference in the content of visual experience

The phenomenal contrast is due exclusively to the difference
between the contents of the visual parts of the target and the contrasting experience, but neither visual experience represents the
target property.

In the causation case, an alternative of this type would say that
instead of differing in whether they represent causal properties,

the two experiences in our example differ in whether they represent certain color and shape (or other non-K) properties.

On what basis could one decide between target explanations and the three alternatives? If we could rely only on introspection to decide between them, then the method of phenomenal contrast would face the same difficulties as the method of introspecting single cases. Hardly anything general can be said about the basis on which to decide between the alternatives at this stage, since the considerations will vary from case to case. They include considering the general plausibility of the alternatives, and considering analogous phenomenal contrasts to see whether it is plausible to suppose that the proposed explanations would apply in those cases as well. We will see a variety of considerations in the chapters that follow.

Someone inclined toward skepticism about the method might worry that none of the alternatives can get any more traction than the others, because the phenomenal contrast—the explanandum—does not place enough constraints on what an explanation of it has to be like. Compare a case in which our explanandum is the rising of mercury in a thermometer, and our competing explanations are (a) that there is a gas heater in the room, and (b) that there is a wood stove in the room. Even together with background facts about how thermometers work, the rising of the mercury does not help us decide between these two hypotheses. A skeptic might worry that hypotheses that arise when we test the Rich Content View are similarly unconstrained by the phenomenal contrast. In such a case, the method won't help us test the Rich Content View.

In reply, I am assuming as a working hypothesis that the phenomenal contrasts will place enough constraints on the Rich Content View and its competitors to be useful in deciding between them. To see how the assumption fares, we have to consider its application in specific cases.

In describing the method of phenomenal contrast, I have focused on an application of the method to test the Rich Content

View. But nothing in the method itself biases it toward the Rich Content View or any other hypothesis. It could just as well be employed to test the thesis that color or shape properties are represented in experience. Whichever theses the method is employed to test, it provides a way to limit the use of introspection in theorizing about visual experience. All that introspection is relied upon to do is to detect the phenomenal contrast. The method need not take a stand on the source of the phenomenal contrast, such as whether it comes from a sensory or a non-sensory part of the overall experience. It also need not take a stand on the underlying structure of the phenomenal states in general, such as whether they ever include raw feels, or whether they are fundamentally propositional attitudes, or perceptual relations to objects. Like the Content View, introspection can leave these issues unresolved. Finally, introspection need not take a stand on whether the phenomenal difference between the experiences in the pair is also a difference in content, let alone on what the difference in content, if there is one, may be. In these ways, what introspection is relied upon to do is minimal.

Let us now see the method of phenomenal contrast at work. In the next three chapters, it is applied to the case of kind properties (in chapter 4) and causal properties (in chapter 5). I'll employ the method one last time in chapter 7 to argue that a pair of relations between the perceiver and the objects she perceives is represented in visual experience.

PART II

PROPERTIES

Which properties are represented in visual experience? Color, shape, illumination, motion, and their co-instantiation in objects are standardly taken to be so represented. Do visual experiences ever represent any properties other than these? In the next two chapters, I argue that some visual experiences do. Equivalently, some such experiences represent K-properties. The thesis to be defended is the Rich Content View.

The Rich Content View: In some visual experiences, some K-properties are represented.

The Rich Content View is a version of the Content View. If the Content View were true but the Rich Content View were false, then the only properties that could be represented in experience would be non-K properties.

Although the Rich Content View is a version of the Content View, something very much like it could be true even if the Content View were false. For instance, suppose that, contrary to the arguments in chapter 2, standard Naïve Realism did not entail the Content View. K-properties could still be presented in experience, by being among the properties with which we can be in perceptual contact when we see objects. K-properties would then figure in experiences as Naïve Realism construes them. The Content View provides a useful framework for discussing the Rich Content View, by clarifying the underlying issue addressed by the Rich Content View. By sacrificing some degree of clarity, however, the issue could be divorced from the framework.

My strategy in part II is to select K-properties that antecedently seem to be especially strong candidates for the Rich Content View, and use the method of phenomenal contrast to test hypotheses about the representation of these properties in experience. If these K-properties can be represented in experience, that makes it somewhat more likely that other K-properties can be represented in experience as well. Using this strategy I will defend the Rich Content View.

Chapter 4

Kinds

K-PROPERTIES ARE DEFINED NEGATIVELY BY EXCLUDING A SMALL class of properties that include color, shape, illumination, and motion. There are thus a great number of K-properties, ranging from properties that categorize objects (person, bicycle, mountain, porch), to those that categorize actions (carrying a dog, climbing a mountain), mental states (feeling sad, being inquisitive, trying to balance on one foot), and words (being a word of Russian, being a phrase that means that the highway exit is just ahead). In this chapter I'll focus mainly on kind properties that categorize objects. We can investigate whether visual experiences represent these K-properties by focusing on cases in which subjects gradually develop recognitional capacities, leading to changes in their beliefs about what they see. We can start with two types of cases in which changes in recognitional dispositions bring about phenomenal changes.

4.1 THE EXAMPLES

The first example involves the disposition to recognize semantic properties of a bit of text, grounded in the knowledge of how to read it. Almost all of us have experienced hearing others speak in a foreign language that we don't understand and that we can't parse into words and sentences. The phenomenology of hearing the same speech when we do understand is markedly different.

This contrast in auditory experiences has a visual analog: consider a page of Cyrillic text. The way it looks to someone before and after she learns to read Russian seems to bring about a phenomenological difference in how the text looks.[1] When you are first learning to read the script of a language that is new to you, you have to attend to each word, and perhaps to each letter, separately. In contrast, once you can easily read it, it takes a special effort to attend to the shapes of the script separately from its semantic properties. You become disposed to attend to the semantic properties of the words in the text, and less disposed to attend to the orthographic ones.

The second example involves a different recognitional disposition. Suppose you have never seen a pine tree before and are hired to cut down all the pine trees in a grove containing trees of many different sorts. Someone points out to you which trees are pine trees. Some weeks pass, and your disposition to distinguish the pine trees from the others improves. Eventually, you can spot the pine trees immediately: they become visually salient to you. Like the recognitional disposition you gain, the salience of the trees emerges gradually. Gaining this recognitional disposition is reflected in a phenomenological difference between the visual experiences had before and those had after the recognitional disposition was fully developed.

The argument for the Rich Content View from these cases has three substantial premises, plus a premise that is unproblematic if the cases are convincing. Let E1 be the visual experience had by a subject S who is seeing the pine trees before learning to recognize them, and let E2 be the visual experience had by S when S sees the pine trees after learning to recognize them. E1 and E2 are visual parts of S's overall experiences at each of these times. The overall experience of which E1 is a part is the contrasting experience, and the overall experience of which E2 is a part is the target experience.

---

1. Peacocke (1992, chapter 3) makes a similar phenomenological claim.

I'm going to call the premise that is unproblematic if the cases are convincing premise (0):

(0) The target experience differs in its phenomenology from the contrasting experience.

Claim (0) is supposed to be an intuition. It is the minimal intuition one has to have for the argument to get off the ground.

(1) If the target experience differs in its phenomenology from the contrasting experience, then there is a phenomenological difference between E1 and E2.
(2) If there is a phenomenological difference between E1 and E2, then E1 and E2 differ in content.
(3) If there is a difference in content between E1 and E2, it is a difference with respect to K-properties represented in E1 and E2.

If no experiences represent K-properties, then there will be no difference between E1 and E2 with respect to K-properties represented in them. So if (3) and its antecedent are true, then the Rich Content View is, too. An analogous argument could be made for the case of the Cyrillic text.

Premises (0) and (1) entail that there is a phenomenological difference between the target and the contrasting experiences. Premise (1) specifies that E1 and E2 differ phenomenally. Premise (0), in contrast, allows that E1 and E2 are phenomenally the same.

Given premise (0), there are three ways to block the inference from these cases of recognitional dispositions to the Rich Content View. First, one could deny that the phenomenological contrast is a contrast between E1 and E2. This would be to deny premise (1). Second, one could grant that E1 and E2 are phenomenally different, but deny that there is any accompanying representational difference (e.g., any difference in contents of E1 and E2). This would be to deny premise (2). Finally, one could grant that E1 and E2 differ in their representational features, but deny that the change involves any representation of K-properties. This would be to deny premise (3). I will consider each of these moves in turn.

4.2 THE PREMISES

Premise (1): Non-Sensory Experiences?

Let me start with the first way of attempting to block the inference to the Rich Content View. There are various kinds of phenomenally conscious states besides sensory states. There are bodily sensations, visual imagery, background experiences (such as moods), and perhaps (as we discussed in 3.3) cognitive experiences. If the phenomenological change described in the two cases is due to a difference with respect to any of these states, the two most plausible suggestions seem to be that it is a change either in some sort of cognitive phenomenology or in background phenomenology. Someone might be tempted to re-describe the text and tree cases so that, as far as visual phenomenology is concerned, the experiences had with and without recognitional dispositions are the same, but the difference in phenomenology of overall experiences is due to a non-sensory factor.[2] If these descriptions were correct, then the examples would not bear on what properties visual experience represents at all, and hence would not bear at all on the Rich Content View.

The strategy of the opponent I'm considering, then, is to re-describe the tree and text cases by invoking non-sensory experiences and thereby avoid making a commitment to the Rich Content View. Let's consider cognitive experiences first.

What structure would such re-descriptions have to have? Well, first, there would have to be a phenomenally conscious state that is distinct from any sensory state. Second, if the non-sensory state involves a propositional attitude of some sort, a plausible account would have to be given of the attitude involved in the event and of the content of that attitude.

---

2. Since we are supposing that no other sensory modalities are involved in representing the property of being a pine tree, we can ignore any non-visual sensory differences between the experiences.

The general idea behind the strategy is that the familiarity that one gains in gaining a recognitional disposition is reflected in cognitive phenomenology. I now want to list some of the options for the types of non-sensory experiences, attitudes, and contents that an opponent of the Rich Content View who followed this strategy might cite to account for this feeling of familiarity. Though the list of options is not meant to be exhaustive, those on it are natural ones to consider. Once they are on the table, it will be easier to assess the case against the Rich Content View.

It is natural to list the states and attitudes together. They include:

   (i) Forming a judgment,
  (ii) Dwelling on a belief,
 (iii) Entertaining a hunch or intuition, and
 (iv) Entertaining a proposition by having it pass through your mind, without committing to its truth.

These are four sorts of occurrent states. Entries (i)–(iii) involve commitment: the attitudes are all related to belief, and an accompanying commitment to the truth of the thing believed. Hunches and intuitions are like beliefs in that the subject accepts their content for certain purposes. For instance, in testing a hypothesis, one may reason as if a hunch or intuition were true. Entry (iv), in contrast, does not involve any such commitment. This distinction will be useful shortly.

What about the content of these states? Since these states are supposed to be brought about in part by gaining a recognitional disposition, the contents should reflect this gain in some way. Some reasonable options include these (I'll stick to the case of the trees):

 (a) *That* is a pine tree (mentally demonstrating a tree).
 (b) I've seen trees with *that look* before.
 (c) I recognize *that kind of tree*.
 (d) *That kind of tree* is familiar.

These are supposed to be contents of mental states rather than contents expressed by actual uses of sentences. As such, the proposal that there are attitudes that have (a)–(d) as contents involves a notion of a demonstrative thought, independent of the notion of what is expressed by an actual use of a demonstrative. The contents are analogs for thought of contents expressed by use of sentences.

Suppose we combine any of these contents into any of the attitudes and states in the first list. Then we will have a candidate for a phenomenally conscious mental state.

Let me now examine one instance of the strategy I've outlined for denying premise (1). In the tree case, the suggestion amounts to this: how the tree looks before and after you become disposed to recognize pine trees is exactly the same; that is, it looks to have certain color and shape properties. But the moment you recognize the tree, you experience a feeling of familiarity, and this feeling accounts for the phenomenological change before and after you gain the disposition. So, on this suggestion the way the tree looks stays the same, before and after you become disposed to recognize it; but the phenomenology of "taking" the tree to be familiar contributes to the phenomenal change accompanying E2. For the purpose of discussion, I'll select the event and attitude of dwelling on a belief, and the content that *that kind of tree* is familiar; that is, (ii) and (d).

I'm going to raise two objections to the view that the phenomenological change in the tree case consists exclusively in a change in a phenomenally conscious mental state with attitude (ii) and content (d). The first objection would also apply if the attitude were (i) or (iii) and if it had any of the four contents listed. My second objection is more general: it would apply to any combination of the events, attitudes, and contents listed.

The first objection focuses on the states with commitment-involving attitudes. Suppose that you're an expert pine-spotter looking at some pine trees in the forest. Then someone tells you that the forest has been replaced by an elaborate hologram, causing you to cease to dwell on the belief that you're looking at a familiar tree. If an event such as (ii) (d) were what contributed to the phenomenological change before and after your acquiring the disposition to recognize pine trees, then we would expect your acceptance of the hologram story to make the hologram look as the forest looked to you before you knew how to recognize pine trees. But, intuitively, the hologram could look exactly the same as the forest looked to you after you became an expert. So the familiarity with pine trees does not seem to have its phenomenological effects at the level of belief.

The case against the proposal that the feeling of familiarity is conferred by a belief holds equally well against the proposal that substitutes any of the commitment-involving events or attitudes for the one I chose for purposes of discussion. Hunches and intuitions, like beliefs, seem to be attitudes that one could lose by accepting the testimony described above. If anything, hunches and intuitions are *less* resistant than beliefs are to counter-evidence—if the belief wouldn't survive one's accepting hologram testimony, then neither would hunches or intuitions.

The objection I've just made would not threaten a version of the strategy that invoked a non-commitment-involving attitude, such as entertaining a proposition without committing to its truth. So let us focus on a version of the proposal that appeals to a mental state of this sort. In this version of the proposal, in the tree case, when you look at the tree after gaining the recognitional disposition, you get into a phenomenally conscious mental state distinct from sensing. This is an event (we're supposing) of entertaining the proposition that *that kind of tree* is familiar, where this proposition passes through your mind without your committing to its truth.

Here it is important to keep in view the aspect of the proposal that posits an occurrent cognitive state. This proposal predicts that there will be a phenomenological difference between your experiences of seeing the pine tree before and after you learn to recognize trees, only to the extent that you're in such an occurrent, phenomenally conscious state. If you're not in such a state, then, this proposal predicts, there will be no phenomenological change of the sort invoked in the original example.

The second objection targets this aspect of the proposal. The occurrent state is something explicit, not akin to having a tacit recognition (or misrecognition) of something as a tree. But the phenomenological change in the original tree example seems to be the sort that does not always involve the explicit entertaining of a proposition such as (d). Consider a comparable example from Charles Siewert:

> Think of how individual people look different to you after you have gotten to know them than they did when you first met. Notice how different your neighborhood looks to you now that you have lived there for a while, than it did on the day you first arrived.[3]

What can happen with a neighborhood, it seems, can happen with trees as well. The phenomenological change is the sort that we can infer by remembering how different things looked before we became familiar with them. Becoming aware of the phenomenon involves thinking of something—a person, a neighborhood, or a kind of object, such as a tree—as familiar. But simply undergoing the phenomenon does not have to involve this. There need not be, it seems, an extra episode (or occurrent state), beyond sensing, for the phenomenological change to take effect.

I've raised this objection to the proposal that invokes a non-commitment-involving attitude. But it works equally well, if it works at all, against the proposal invoking a commitment-involving attitude.

At this point, the denier of premise (1) might reply to the objection by claiming that the cognitive state in question could have a

---

3. Siewert (1998), p. 257–258. Cf. Fleming (1957): "We speak of the experience of recognition, and sometimes, when we say that we recognize something, we mean to refer to a change in the character or quality of our experience: what we recognize looks different after we recognize it from the way it looked before" (161).

content such as (d) explicitly, without being an occurrent state of the sort I've described. After all, the denier might point out, sensory experience has its content explicitly, without involving something analogous to *saying* to oneself something like (d) (e.g., "well, how about that; that's a tree").

If the putatively non-sensory event does not involve something analogous to saying to oneself something like (d), and if it is supposed to be something other than an event of visually appearing, then it becomes less clear that it is phenomenally conscious at all.

Let me now consider the proposal that the phenomenal change is a change in background phenomenology, rather than a change in an occurrent cognitive state. Someone who denied premise (1) might claim that although the phenomenological difference between E1 and E2 is not sensory, neither does it belong to a specific occurrent cognitive state.

Drunkenness and depression may be two examples of standing, background states that affect overall experience. As against premise (1), someone might claim that recognitional dispositions are like drunkenness and depression in the crucial respect: they, too, are standing states of a subject that can affect overall phenomenology—and, indeed, the objector will claim, that is just what happens in the text and the tree cases.

Now, to defeat premise (1) in this way, what the objector would need is a reason to think that changes in standing states can affect overall phenomenology in some way other than by causing changes in sensory phenomenology. Depression and drunkenness may involve at least some such changes: depression causes things to look gray; drunkenness causes them to look blurry. The relevant analogy has to be between changes in overall phenomenology that are not the result of changes in sensory phenomenology. The changes must be akin to changes in mood.

Having a recognitional disposition, however, is not phenomenologically like being in a mood at all. Moods have relatively non-local effects on phenomenology: almost nothing seems exciting

during depression; nearly everything seems exciting during drunkenness. In contrast, being disposed to recognize pine trees does not
have such overall phenomenological effects. So whatever phenomenal change results from gaining recognitional dispositions, it does
not seem to be a change in background phenomenology.

Let me now consider how the text example fares if (1) is false
and the phenomenological difference in how text looks before and
after one learns to read it is a difference in cognitive, as opposed
to sensory, phenomenology.

A fan of premise (1) can grant that there are some cases in
which reading a text does involve undergoing events that have
a phenomenology and that are arguably non-sensory. Lingering
on a sentence while deliberating about whether it is true has a
phenomenology, and arguably such an event is non-sensory. Such
a thing could happen, for instance, if you weren't perceiving
anything at all but were simply entertaining the proposition
expressed by the sentence.

Contrast this phenomenology with that of being bombarded by
pictures and captions on billboards along the highway. This seems
a visual analog of the blare of a loud television, or a fellow pas-
senger's inane cell-phone conversation: understanding the text on
the billboard as you drive by isn't a deliberate affair; rather (if the
billboards have been positioned correctly), it just happens. The
advertisers would doubtless be happy if you lingered over every
billboard's message, but no such event need occur in order for
you to take in the semantic properties of the text as you whiz by.
This suggests that the taking in can be merely sensory.

So far, I've considered two ways to deny (1). One way is to propose that the phenomenal change is a change in cognitive phenomenology that is attached to a specific event in the stream of
consciousness. The other way is to propose that the phenomenal
change is a change in background phenomenology. I've given reasons to think neither of these ways of denying premise (1) in the
argument for Thesis K will succeed. I now turn to the strategy of
denying premise (2).

Premise (2): Raw feels?

The opponent of premise (2) tries to block the inference from the examples of phenomenological change to the Rich Content View by claiming that the phenomenological changes are unaccompanied by any representational change at all.

Premise (2) is a consequence of the more general claim that *any* phenomenal change is a change in content of the phenomenal character of a sensory experience. But premise (2) itself is much more limited. It just makes a claim about the phenomenal change in our pair of cases.

If (2) is false, then there is such a thing as a nonrepresentational feeling of familiarity. This could be part of sensory experience, or part of some sort of cognitive experience. Either way, it would be a feeling of familiarity that could be had even in the absence of perceiving, or seeming to perceive, anything as being familiar. It would not represent anything as being familiar but rather would be akin to a sensory affliction. It would be a raw feel. The proposal is not that there is merely a nonrepresentational *aspect* to a representation of familiarity. Rather, the proposal is that the feeling of familiarity is entirely nonrepresentational.

Against this idea, my defense of (2) is that familiarity is not the sort of thing that can be felt without any representation of something as familiar. The best attempt to make the case for the contrary ends up positing a representation of familiarity after all.

One would expect a raw feeling of familiarity, if there were such a thing, to leave one with a sense of confusion, since if it were clear to the subject what was being felt to be familiar, then this would seem to make the feeling representational after all. Suppose, for example, you see someone who acts toward you as a stranger would, and this seems inappropriate to you, but you can't at first figure out why. In response to this feeling of strangeness, you might think to ask the person whether you have met before. But the feeling you have that leads you to ask it, someone might suggest, is a raw feeling of familiarity. It is a variety of "déjà vu."

In the case above, the sense of confusion comes from the fact that though you take the person to be familiar, you don't recognize who they are. There are two aspects to this experience: you represent something as familiar without recognizing it; and you represent something as familiar without at first realizing that it is so represented. The first aspect is definitive of déjà vu: a place, a sound, or a situation strikes you as familiar, without your being able to discern what is familiar about it. This is simply a less specific representation of familiarity; it is not a case of a feeling that does not represent anything as familiar. So the putative case of a raw feeling of familiarity does not illustrate this after all. And if that case doesn't illustrate it, it is hard to see what kind of case would.

Premise (3): Exclusively Non-K Representation?

I now consider the third response to the argument for the Rich Content View, which is to deny that E1 and E2 differ with respect to the K-properties (if any) that they represent.

Both the tree and the text examples involve a gain in recognitional dispositions, and it will be useful to keep in mind what sort of structure recognition has. A perceiver who can recognize trees by sight seems to have some sort of memory representation, and some sort of perceptual input, such that the input "matches" the memory representation, and the cognitive system of the perceiver registers that this is so. Empirical theories of object recognition are supposed to explain the nature of each of these components (the memory, the input, and the matching), and the mechanisms that underlie them. Part of what's at issue in the debate about the Rich Content View is whether visual experience is only ever an input to such processes of recognition, or whether it can also be an output of such processes. Whichever empirical and philosophical theories turn out to be correct, some structure such as this seems built into the very notion of recognition.

One sort of proposal about the contents of E2 that a denier of premise (3) might invoke would involve the notion of a pine-tree-shape gestalt. Suppose that when you learn to recognize pine trees by sight, your experience comes to represent a complex of shapes— leaf shape, trunk shape, branch shape, and overall pine-tree shape. This complex is an overall pine-tree gestalt. The pine-tree-shape gestalt is general enough that it can be shared by different-looking pine trees. But it is specific enough to capture the look shared by exemplary pine trees. The pine-tree-shape gestalt is invariant across differences in the shape of particular pine trees.

For an experience of seeing a tree to represent a pine-tree-shape gestalt, it need not be part of the content of experience that the tree seen is similar to other trees with respect to specific shapes. It is enough simply to represent the respects in which various pine trees are in fact similar. A pine-tree-shape gestalt, then, is not by definition something that can be represented in experience only if the subject is disposed to believe that the different things instantiating it are the same shape. But all things that have this gestalt have a complex shape-property in common.

It seems plausible to suppose that pine trees share a pine-tree-shape gestalt, to the extent that pine trees, varied though they may be in size and other features, have some quite general shape-properties in common. If there were such a thing as a tree-shape gestalt, then the denier of (3) could invoke this as the non-K property that E2 represents and E1 doesn't. I'm going to call this proposal for denying (3) Shape-Gestalt.

> Shape-Gestalt: E1 and E2 differ with respect to the pine-tree-shape-gestalt properties they represent, and neither represents any K-properties.

In the tree case, as Shape-Gestalt would describe it, the perceiver's experiences come to represent the tree-shape-gestalt as part of the same process by which the perceiver comes to have a memory representation "matching" that shape-gestalt.

I don't know of a knock-down argument against Shape-Gestalt. But shape-gestalts that are abstract enough to remain invariant across pine trees will be invariant across other objects as well. For

instance, a typical handgun, a drill, and a hair dryer share the
same shape-gestalt. The more abstract a shape-gestalt is, the less
reason there is to think that experience fails to represent it prior to
one's gaining a recognitional disposition. And if it is represented
in experience prior to gaining the recognitional disposition, then
it cannot explain the phenomenal contrast.

In addition, the strategy of invoking the representation-
invariant color-shape complexes to underpin phenomenological
changes does not seem generally available. Consider, for example,
the property of a face expressing doubt. One could learn to recognize when the face of someone, call him X, was expressing doubt.
X might even belong to a group of people whose faces all express
doubt in the same way. Initially, one might not know that X and
his kin were expressing doubt when they looked that way. But
this is something one could learn to recognize by observing them.
In this sort of case, it seems implausible to suppose that there
must be a change in which color and shape properties are represented before and after one learns that it is doubt that the face so
contorted expresses. One could initially wonder what the contortion of the face meant, and come to believe that it is an expression
of doubt only after repeated sightings of it and interaction with
the person. This change in interpretation seems to be one that
could be accompanied by a phenomenological change as well.

Once they are adjusted to be about the face case, the other two
premises of the argument still seem to remain true. Exactly the
same considerations apply in the case of premise (2). In premise
(1), the argument for ruling out non-sensory phenomenology also
seems to go through as before, but in the face case an alternative
to sensory phenomenology seems relevant—namely, emotional
phenomenology. Here, it seems possible in principle that X could
learn to detect a look of doubt on Y's face without X's having any
emotional response. Y might be a talking head on television who
lacks any significance for X and triggers no emotional responses.

As for premise (3), an opponent who granted the initial intuition that there is some phenomenal change accompanying the

gain of a recognitional disposition might say that the phenomenal change is sensory but that the novel phenomenology is associated merely with coming to represent the property of being a familiar expression. This option seems to be ruled out by considering a variant of the face case involving two subjects. Consider a counterfactual situation in which X contorts his face in exactly the same way, but in which that contortion expresses bemusement rather than doubt. One could come to learn that it expresses bemusement in the same way as in the first case, by extended observation and interaction. But it seems plausible to suppose that the phenomenal change in each case would be different: one sort of phenomenology for recognizing the doubtful expression, and another sort for recognizing bemusement.

Finally, return to the text example to see how it fares with respect to premise (3). The original intuition was that before and after you learn to read Russian, the same page of Cyrillic text will look different to you. You might love the look of Cyrillic script, keep a page nearby at all times, and study its shapes carefully. Then, after learning to read Russian, you see by reading it that it is a page of insults. Even if you attended to the colors and shapes of the Cyrillic script as thoroughly as possible before learning to read it, you could still experience the page differently once it became intelligible to you.

I've argued that gaining a disposition to recognize K-properties can make a difference to visual phenomenology and that this difference is accompanied by a representation of K-properties in visual experience.

4.3 CONTENT EXTERNALISM

My case for the Rich Content View has proceeded without appealing to any specific theory of intentionality for experiences. However, the pine-tree example might be taken to suggest that one of the K-properties that visual experiences can represent is the natural kind property of being a pine tree. Since it is widely held that any mental state that represents natural kind properties has contents that are externally determined, it is natural to ask what relation the Rich Content View bears to the thesis that some experiential contents are externally determined.

Externalism about experience content is the view that physical duplicates can differ in which contents their experiences have. Since the Rich Content View is silent on what makes it the case that experiences represent what they do, it is clearly compatible with externalism about experience content.

Suppose that the Rich Content View is made true by visual experience representing natural kind properties, such as the property of being a pine tree. And suppose one accepts externalism. It is open to someone who accepts both of these claims to hold that physical duplicates whose environments differ (where only one includes pine trees) have the same visual phenomenology. This would entail that the property of having that visual phenomenology is not identical with the property of representing the property of being a pine tree in experience. But it is compatible with the view that that visual phenomenology supervenes on the contents of visual experience.

The Rich Content View is also compatible with the denial of externalism. Even if one accepts that natural kind properties can be represented in visual experience only if externalism about experience content holds, one need not accept such externalism in order to accept the Rich Content View, because the Rich Content View can be true even if natural kind properties are not represented in experience.

Consider the case discussed earlier, involving dispositions to recognize pine trees. If one rejects externalism but accepts that E2 in the example is an experience that represents some K-property, one has two options. First, one can hold (contrary to the received view) that the property of being a pine tree can be represented even by someone who has never been in contact with pine trees. Second, one can hold that the K-property that comes to be represented in E2 is not the property of being a pine tree, but a more general K-property (possibly a kind property that is not a natural kind property) that both pine trees and superficially similar trees share.

In sum, although the Rich Content View is compatible with externalism about the contents of experience, it does not require it. The argument for the Rich Content View does not appeal to any theses about content-determination. Depending on which such theses one accepts, however, and depending on views about the exact relation between content and phenomenology, one may reach a different verdict on exactly what K-property would come to be represented in the pine-tree example (assuming that the rest of the argument for the Rich Content View were accepted).

If the Rich Content View is true, then it seems reasonable to expect that K-properties other than the property of being a pine tree (or some more general K-property) and the semantic properties of texts are represented in visual experience. The conclusion could be generalized beyond the two specific properties used as examples in the argument by running an exactly analogous argument for other cases in which becoming sensitive to property instances has an effect on overall phenomenology. The argument structure leaves open, however, whether analogous considerations will always be available. Alternatively, the conclusion could be generalized by considering other arguments from phenomenal contrast that do not depend specifically on the gaining of a recognitional disposition to generate the phenomenal contrast. In the next chapter, I employ the method of phenomenal contrast to argue that causal properties are represented in visual experience.

Chapter 5

The Visual Experience of Causation

5.1 THE CAUSAL THESIS

IN THIS CHAPTER, I DEFEND THE CAUSAL THESIS, WHICH ENTAILS THE Rich Content View.

Causal Thesis: Some visual experiences represent causal relations.

What is a causal relation? Consider the relations of pushing, pulling, lifting, stopping, moving, supporting, hanging-from, and preventing something from happening. These might naturally be considered modes of causation: they are specific ways to cause something else to happen. There also seems to be a more general relation that these relations exemplify—causation itself. There may be relations that are less specific than the "modes" I have listed but more specific than causation itself—such as the varieties of mechanical causation discussed by Albert Michotte.[1] In plain launching, an object A approaches a stationary object B, which upon contact starts to move in the same direction in which A was moving. In launching-by-entraining, A pushes B along. In launching-by-expulsion, B moves as if thrown by A.[2] Michotte distinguished mechanical causation from qualitative causation, which need not involve continuity of motion between the apparent cause and apparent effect. The Causal Thesis should be interpreted as saying

1. Michotte (1963/1946).
2. Readers are encouraged to view the demonstrations at http://www.yale.edu/perception/animacy, since it will be useful to keep them vividly in mind for the subsequent discussion.

that visual experiences represent either the more general relation, or one of its specific modes.

Whenever causal relations are represented in a visual experience, the experience will have accuracy conditions and so will represent that such-and-such is the case, where a causal relation R is part of such-and-such. This raises the question of what the relata of the causal relation are. The Causal Thesis leaves this open. The contents of an experience illustrating the Causal Thesis could be naturally (albeit approximately) expressed by a sentence of the form *x causes y to happen*, in which case *y* would be an event. Or the contents could be naturally expressed by a sentence of the form *x R's y*, which posits a relation between two things—sometimes objects ("Bob lifted Jack," "The laundry hangs on the line"), sometimes events ("The scream caused the shudder"). Still another option would be contents roughly expressed by a sentence of the form *x causes y to phi* ("Bob caused Jack to fall," "The scream caused me to shudder"), where *y* and *phi* are pairs of objects and properties that bear some close relation to events. If you applied a systematic semantic theory to each of these sentences, it would posit different truth-conditions for each of them, involving different ontological commitments.

The Causal Thesis is neutral as to which of these contents visual experiences have when they represent causal relations. Such experiences may not always be sensitive to these differences in accuracy conditions, so that there is sometimes some indeterminateness in how exactly the world must be, if the experience is accurate. In other cases, experiences may have more determinate accuracy conditions. All that matters for the Causal Thesis, however, is that the contents include a causal relation.

One might think the Causal Thesis is supported by experiments done by Michotte, who asked adults to describe scenes of launching and entraining, and found that they described them in causal terms. However, the matter is not quite so straightforward. Let us consider more closely how these results bear on the Causal Thesis.

5.2 MICHOTTE'S RESULTS

In the 1940s Michotte published the results of about 150 experiments that showed that adults are inclined to describe scenes of launching and entraining in causal terms. Michotte's experiments were attempts to isolate the exact parameters of motion that elicited such descriptions from adults. In some of the experiments the "objects" were lights or shadows projected on a screen, and in others they were ordinary hefty objects such as wooden balls; some experiments combined both. Many subjects knew that no actual causal relations were instantiated in the situations they saw (such as the case where a shadow "launches" a ball or vice versa), but that did not prevent them from describing what they saw in causal terms. The prevalence of such causal descriptions led Michotte to posit a representation of causality on the part of the adults that was something other than a belief about what was happening in the environment. He called it an "impression of causation."[3] Michotte's results establish that adults regularly describe launching and entraining in causal terms, by saying things such as "the red square moved the blue square along," or "the ball pushed the shadow." What's controversial among psychologists is the nature of the representation underlying the description: Is it learned or innate? Is it specific to the kinetic mechanical domain? Or is it the output of a more general sensitivity to other (or to all) situations that adults classify as causal—perhaps a capacity to keep track of conditional dependencies, including such things as exposure to sun causing skin to redden, or too many hours of sitting in the same position causing one's leg to fall asleep?[4] To what extent are ascriptions of

3. Sometimes psychologists use the term "perceptual causation" to label the kinds of scenes that adults are prone to describe as causal—launching, entraining, or expulsion. Other times "perceptual causation" is used to refer to the kind of mental representation that Michotte posited to explain this description.

4. For a discussion, see Fodor (2006, chap. 2), Gopnik et al. (2004), and Saxe and Carey (2006).

causality sensitive to the intrinsic features of the relata? There is no agreement yet about the correct answers to these questions, and I am not relying on any answers to them here.

For our purposes two questions about Michotte's results are relevant. First, is there any reason to think that the reports that Michotte elicited are reports of visual experience? Second, what if anything do those reports tell us about the contents of the visual experiences that subjects have when they see the displays?

The fact that adults describe situations that they know not to be causal in causal terms does not by itself show that they are reporting a feature of their experience, as opposed to an impression of some other sort. In principle, there could be cognitively insulated pretendings-that-p, which would not be specifically perceptual. Nonetheless, there is prima facie reason to take Michotte's data to tell us something about adults' visual experiences. There is a pattern of motion that regularly elicits causal descriptions—something we would expect to find if they were reporting the contents of visual experience. In contrast, though there could in principle be pretendings that were regularly elicited from the environment, cases of pretense do not regularly have that feature.

This brings us to the second question: what if anything do Michotte's results tell us about the contents of the visual experiences his subjects report?

In general, the way people report what they see is a poor guide to the contents of their visual experience. People may use different expressions to describe a scene that looks the same way—for instance, two people might try to guess how large or how far away something is and differ in how good they are at making such estimations. Taking their reports as a guide would force us to conclude that the table looks to be a different size and different distances away from each subject, when in fact there might be no such differences at all. So if Michotte's results tell us anything about the contents of his subjects' visual experiences, this will not be because we can simply read the contents off their reports. In general, one can't do that.

Michotte's results do not by themselves entail the Causal Thesis. At best, they entail it when combined with further theoretical assumptions about the relation between experience, beliefs, and reports. Consider a case of launching when the "launching" object (sometimes called the "motor object") is a ball, and the "launched" object is (and looks to be) a flash of light. Adults know that hefty objects can't cause flashes of light to move. Now suppose we take the following substantive assumption as a rough guide to the contents of experience: those contents are the contents of what one would believe if one relied on what one knows about the relata. That assumption would allow us to deny the Rich Content View, as the contents of the experience would then be roughly that there is a certain pattern of continuous motion between the ball and the "moving" flash. If we changed the substantive assumption so that the guide to the contents of experience was instead what one would believe if one bracketed what one knows about the nature of the relata, then we might get a different result—that the ball causes the flash to move, which entails the Rich Content View. Either way, we would get a verdict that bears on the Causal Thesis only when Michotte's results are combined with substantive theoretical assumptions linking reports to background beliefs and contents of experience.

One could try to argue for the Causal Thesis by finding a principle relating "report contents" and "experience contents" in a way that can be added to Michotte's results to support the Causal Thesis.[5] But instead of trying to develop such a principle here, let us see how far we can get using the method of phenomenal contrast.

5.3 UNITY IN EXPERIENCE

Suppose there is a cat sitting on a loose-mesh hammock, forming a sitting-cat-shaped dip in the hammock's surface. The Causal Thesis allows that your experience of seeing the cat represents that the cat is pressing the hammock downward. If the Causal

5. For a discussion of potential difficulties with this strategy, see Schwitzgebel (2007).

Thesis is false, then your experience can represent that the part of the hammock directly under the cat is closer to the ground than the rest of it, but not that the cat is pressing down on it. The opponent of the Causal Thesis holds that experience simply remains neutral on whether any force is being continuously exerted in such a case.

The opponent's description of the cat-hammock experience does not strike me as phenomenologically apt. But the phenomenological aptitude of a proposed content for visual experience can be hard to judge when we are given only a single case. Given only a single case, it can be difficult to discern what the phenomenal character of the visual experience is and, hence, hard to discern which contents most adequately reflect it. Instead, I will discuss two pairs of experiences that differ phenomenally and will use the method of phenomenal contrast to decide whether the Causal Thesis is true.

The pairs of experiences to which the method will be applied involve qualitative causation rather than mechanical causation of the sort for which Michotte proposed input conditions that trigger causal representations. Our cases bring into focus a specific and familiar kind of unity in experience. Suppose that you are playing catch indoors. A throw falls short and the ball lands with a thump in a potted plant, with its momentum absorbed all at once by the soil. You see it land, and just after that the lights go out. The ball's landing in the plant does not cause the lights to go out, and let us suppose that you don't believe that it does. Nonetheless, it may seem to you that the ball's landing somehow caused the lights to go out. Call this the target experience. Like our other target experiences, it is an overall conscious experience that includes a visual experience. In the second case, you see the ball land and the lights go out. But unlike the target experience, this experience does not involve any feeling that the ball's landing *caused* the lights to go out. Call this the contrasting experience. The visual part of the contrasting experience represents the ball's trajectory and its landing, and it represents the lights going out, but so far as your visual experience is concerned, these events merely occur in quick succession.

It seems plain that there can be a phenomenal difference between two such experiences. This provides a starting point for the method described above. But in this case, a bit more can be said at the outset about the phenomenal contrast to be explained. This contrast seems to have something to do with the connection between events: the difference stems from how the lights' going off seems to you to be related to the landing of the ball.[6] The successive events seem to be unified in experience in a way that is not merely temporal.

There are also cases of a similar sort of experienced unity involving simultaneous events. Suppose that you open a curtain and let in some light. Here there is one event (the uncovering of the window) that occurs simultaneously with another event (the increased illumination of the room). They can also, let us assume, be experienced as occurring simultaneously. Contrast this with a case in which you open a curtain that does not block out any light in the first place (perhaps because it is translucent). Just as you uncover the window, the sun comes out from behind a dark cloud, causing the room to lighten progressively as the curtain is opened. Here we have a very similar event of uncovering the window, coupled with an event of the room gradually lightening, and (we can suppose) these events have and are experienced as having the same duration. But it seems that there could nonetheless be a phenomenal difference between the two experiences, with respect

6. I've focused on how the observed events seem to be related: the lights going off seems related to the trajectory of the ball. Arguably, the associated experiences (or parts of experience) also seem to be related: the experience of seeing the lights go off seems related to the experience of seeing the ball land in the plant. I'm setting aside the question of how these two kinds of unity (experienced unity among things represented, and unity of experiences) may be related.

to how the window's uncovering and the room's illumination are experienced as related to one another. I'm taking this to be an intuition. In this application of the method for investigating whether a certain content is a content of visual experience, I'm taking the explanandum to be not merely a phenomenal contrast but, more specifically, a contrast with respect to whether the events in question seem to be unified—leaving open, at the outset, just what kind of unity those events seem to have.

In what way might the events seem to be unified? A natural suggestion is that, in the one case, there is an experiential representation of causation, whereas in the other case, there is not. If this is so, then in the ball case, one of the experiences represents the ball's landing and the lights going off as causally unified; and in the curtain case, one of the experiences represents that the uncovering of the window lets in the light. The main motivation of the Causal Thesis is that it provides a plausible account of the phenomenal difference between the target and the contrasting experience in each pair.

To properly defend the Causal Thesis, what is needed are reasons to think this is the best account of the phenomenal contrast. As in our discussion of kinds in the previous chapter, here we can identify three hypotheses.

> **Non-sensory experiences:** The target experience includes a phenomenally conscious non-sensory state, and the phenomenal contrast is explained by the absence of this non-sensory state in the contrasting experience.
>
> **Raw feels:** One of the experiences involves a raw feel that the other one lacks.
>
> **Non-causal contents:** The target and contrasting experiences include visual experiences that differ in their contents, but the contents of both visual experiences are exclusively non-causal, and the phenomenal contrast is explained by a contrast in non-causal contents.

I'll consider these hypotheses in reverse order.

5.4 NON-CAUSAL CONTENTS

We are starting from the assumption that there is a phenomenal difference between the target experience and the contrasting experience in each pair (the ball case, and the curtain case). According to the hypothesis of non-causal contents, this difference is a difference exclusively in the non-causal contents of the visual part of each experience. The central question about this proposal is whether the contents of each of the visual experiences in question could be exclusively non-causal.

Let us focus for a moment on motion, illumination, and temporal contiguity in the curtain case. An opponent of the Causal Thesis might say that if the two events—the uncovering and the lightening—unfold in such a way that the increase in light is correlated with the movement of the curtain in just the right way, then there will be an impression of unity between these events. But this need not be an impression of causal unity, the opponent might say—it is merely an impression of a special correlation between the rates at which two things happen.

Could it be the rate at which the window is uncovered and light streams in that makes it seem as if uncovering the window has let in the light? If so, then while these rates could be the same in each of the curtain cases, they could not be visually represented as the same—since if they were, then (according to this proposal) there would be an impression of causation in both cases, whereas by hypothesis there is such an impression in only one of them.

This opponent of the Causal Thesis thus has to hold that if there were a pair of curtain experiences with the phenomenal difference described, one of the experiences would have to be falsidical. The same would apply in the ball case.

This prediction seems implausible. Why must either experience involve any error in how fast the uncovering or the lightening is experienced as occurring? Taken separately, each case in the pair can perfectly well be imagined to be a completely veridical experience. So this alternative requires illusion where intuitively, there does not seem to have to be any. If there need not be any such illusion, then both the actual rates of the events and the rates at which they are experienced as occurring can be the same both times. It seems that the opponent of the Causal Thesis will have to look elsewhere to account for the phenomenal difference.

Where else might they look? The curtain cases were described in such a way that the color and thickness of the curtain differ in the scenes, and there were corresponding differences in the contents of experience. The difference in perceived color, however, seems irrelevant to experienced unity between the uncovering of the window and the lightening of the room. Changing the perceived color of the curtain would not seem to affect whether or not the visual experience represents the light as being let in as a result of the curtain's moving, so long as the curtain were thick. (Moreover, if one could have such an experience at all, it seems that one could have it without even registering the color of the curtain.) What about the curtain? Let's suppose—purely for the sake of argument—that the curtain's luminous properties are unlike its color, in that at least one of the experiences has to represent the status of the curtain as either opaque or transparent. (That leaves open whether or not the other experience is neutral on the curtain's luminous properties, either by failing to represent anything about them at all, or by representing a more general luminous property, of which opacity and translucence are determinates.) Now consider the claim that the phenomenal difference between the two curtain-opening cases is due to a difference in representation of luminous properties. In effect, it proposes to explain an impression of unity between the window-uncovering and the room's getting lighter by focusing exclusively on the illumination properties of the curtain itself.

If the impression of unity has any content at all, however, then it would concern the relation between the lightening and the uncovering of the window—since these are the events that seem to be unified. This proposal looks for the key representational element in a different relational property—the relation between the curtain and light in general. So it seems to be looking in the wrong place.

Another option is that visual experience represents the events in question as unified without representing them as *causally* unified. What kind of unity then might characterize them? Perhaps there is a kind of unity analogous to Husserl's notion of *retention*. Suppose you hear a series of five sounds: the clink of a cup against a saucer, the groan of an accelerating bus, a creak from a chair, a snippet of a loud voice, and the honk of a car's horn. Compare this auditory experience to hearing five notes of a melody. We experience the notes of the melody as unified in a way that we need not experience the five sounds as unified—even if at each moment we remember the sounds from the previous moments. Husserl observed that such remembering does not suffice to make us experience any remembered series of motley sounds as being integrated in the same way that we hear the notes of a melody as integrated. Rather, when we hear the sounds as a melody, the previous ones remain present to us in a distinctive way even after they have ceased. Husserl introduced a special term for this way that something remains present to us: *retention*. In the case of the melody, the previous notes are retained, whereas in the series of motley sounds they are not, and that is why we hear the notes, but not the motley sounds, as a melody.[7]

There seems to be a phenomenal difference between these two experiences, and one that stems not just from the different qualities of the individual sounds but from the way those sounds seem to be related to one another in each experience. One might think that, analogously, the ball's landing in the plant seems in the first case to be unified with the lights' going out, while it does not seem that way in the second case. The general idea seems to be that the events somehow belong together as a unit—perhaps in

7. Husserl ([1893]1980) discusses the notion of retention in connection with hearing.

something like the way the Gestalt psychologists thought that the geese in a flock appear to be a unit.

As stated, this proposal isn't very specific. Going with that, it is not clear what accuracy conditions it is positing. Likewise, in the case of retention, it is difficult to say how the world has to be in order for experiences of retention to be accurate. It is clearly not enough that the notes of the melody occur in succession. The opponent of the Causal Thesis we've been considering wants to draw an analogy between retention, on the one hand, and a kind of unity that can be visually represented in the case of the ball or the curtain, on the other, where the unity experiences have exclusively non-causal contents. That raises the question of which contents these are. To get a proposal that we can assess, it needs to say, at a minimum, how things in the world have to be in order for the experience to be accurate.

Return to the case of the ball's landing in the plant and appearing to turn off the lights. Let's suppose that the ball's landing doesn't really turn off the light. So the proponent of the causal thesis (if she agrees that this experience illustrates the thesis) predicts that the experience is falsidical, because it represents two events as causally related when they are not. What does the opponent predict about the experience? Is it veridical because the events are really unified in the way that experience presents them as being (and there is no other illusion), or is it falsidical because the events only appear to be unified? A similar question applies to the experience of seeing the light coming on at 6 a.m. and then hearing the neighbor's whirring coffee grinder. There does not seem to be any relation holding between events in the world that determines whether such experiences are falsidical. This suggests to me that the analogy with Husserlian retention should not be taken to suggest that there is non-causal unity content in the curtain and ball cases. The lesson of the analogy should just be that there is a special kind of temporal relation that one can experience events as having, and sometimes such events also seem to be causally related, but at other times they don't.

How else might one try to account for the feeling of unity in the ball and curtain cases (and others like them), without accepting the causal thesis? A more specific proposal is that in the ball case, the experience represents that if the ball had not landed in the plant, then the lights would not have gone out. According to this proposal, what is represented is a relation of counterfactual dependence; specifically, the lights' going out counterfactually depends on the ball's landing in the plant.

Now, some philosophers think that causation is a kind of counterfactual dependence, and they may hear this proposal as a proposal in favor of the Causal Thesis, rather than as a proposed alternative to it. But even those who favor counterfactual analyses of causation do not identify this relation with causation itself. For example, according to Lewis, if c and e are two events such that e would not have occurred without c, then c is a cause of e—so counterfactual dependence is sufficient for causation. But he denies that it is necessary. Others who have developed counterfactual theories of causation take counterfactual dependence as a starting point, rather than as a stopping point of analysis. Because it has struck many philosophers as such a reasonable starting point for analyses of causation, one might think that it is the perfect candidate for being a non-causal relation that is represented in experience: it is (relatively) simple but close enough (by their lights) to causation itself to promise to account for unity phenomenology in the cases at issue.

More generally, the proposal says that for two events x, y that occur, if an experience represents that y would not have occurred had x not occurred, then it will seem to the subject as if x and y are unified in the way that the ball's landing and the lights going off seem to be unified. This proposal predicts that if visual experience represents that an event y counterfactually depends on an event x then those events will be experienced as unified in the way exemplified by the ball and the curtain cases.

Some philosophers think that counterfactuals cannot be represented in visual experience. Colin McGinn seems to voice this claim here: "You do not see what would obtain in certain counter-factual situations; you see only what actually obtains. When you see something as red you do not see the counterfactual possibil-ities that constitute its having a disposition to appear red. Your eyes do not respond to woulds and might have beens."[8] There are several different things McGinn might have in mind. One is that we do not see events other than the actual ones that occur at the time of the experience. This is true. Another claim is that if you see that an object has a property F, then F has to be instantiated by the object you see. This claim is also true. But it does not follow from either of these claims that it is impossible to see that an object has a dispositional property. If a thing has a disposition, then it is part of "what actually obtains" that the thing has the disposition. If a counterfactual is true of an object you see, then the counterfactual is part of what actually obtains, too.

A different thing McGinn might have in mind is simply that counterfactuals cannot be represented in visual experience—not because they are not part of what actually obtains, but because their antecedents and consequents describe occurrences that are not occurring in the very situation being seen (or, in the case of a hallucination, in the situation that is experientially represented). If this claim is true, then the proposal that instead of representing causal relations between the ball landing and the lights going off, the subject's experience represents that the lights going off coun-terfactually depends on the ball landing will be false.

I think the proposal is false, but not because counterfactuals in general cannot be represented in visual experience. J. J. Gibson suggested that we sometimes perceive "affordances" of things, where these are possibilities for interaction with them—such as that a ball is rollable, or that a flat solid surface would support us, or that we will not find support beyond a "cliff" where the floor suddenly drops off.[9] If we can perceive affordances, then there

8. McGinn (1996).
9. Gibson and Walk (1960).

will be cases where we can perceive possible—and sometimes merely possible—continuations of what we actually see. Perhaps one of the simplest cases of such an affordance would be a ball's continuing along the path on which it was thrown. If someone catches it, then she interrupts its path, and arguably there are cases (curveball aside) in which we can perceive and experientially represent the direction in which it would have continued had it not been caught. More exactly, we can experientially represent that the ball would have continued in the direction it was moving, had its path not been interrupted. Consider some other examples: you see someone trying to grab hold of a cup sitting on a high shelf. He stands on his toes, stretching one arm up as high as it will go, straining to reach a bit higher. But the cup is just out of reach. In the counterfactual *if he reached just a bit farther, he could grab the cup*, the antecedent describes the continuation of a motion that one can see—the motion of reaching for the cup. Similarly, suppose you are watching a powerful windstorm, with wind blowing so hard that a cloth stuck to a tree branch is waving furiously and remains attached to the branch only by a small corner. The antecedent of the counterfactual *if the wind blew harder, the cloth would fly away* describes a strengthening of the wind. One can imagine a rock balancing precariously on the pointed tip of another rock. Could your visual experience represent that if the person reached just a bit farther, he could grab the cup, or that if the wind blew harder, the cloth would fly away, or that if the rock were pushed, it would tip over? As proposals about the contents of the visual experience, these are not obviously incorrect. If these counterfactuals can be represented in visual experience, then McGinn goes too far if he suggests that no counterfactuals can be so represented.

Nonetheless, there is something correct in McGinn's doubt that counterfactuals can be represented in experience. McGinn seems correct about the case in which the antecedent of the counterfactual does not specify any natural continuation of an event that you see. Return to the cases of the ball and the curtain. In the ball case, it is the event of the ball's landing and the event of the lights' going off that seem to be unified. So if the proposal challenging the Causal Thesis by appealing to counterfactual dependence were correct, then we should expect that the visual experience in this case represents that if the ball had not landed in the plant, then the lights would not have gone off. In the curtain case, it is the event of moving the curtain, and the lightening of the room that seem to be unified. So if the proposal were correct, we should expect that the subject's visual experience represents that if the curtain had not moved, the room would not have lightened.

In both of these counterfactuals, the antecedents do not describe natural continuations or movements of scenes that the subject sees. Instead, the antecedents merely negate a description of something that happens, without any indication of what would have happened instead. The reason to think that this could not be represented in visual experience derives from the intuition that McGinn voices when he says that our eyes do not respond to woulds and might-have-beens. The antecedent of the counterfactuals in the ball and curtain cases are not closely enough connected to what the subject actually sees to be represented in visual experience. The possibilities they describe are visually unconnected with the actual events that one sees. The hypothesis that we represent counterfactual dependence in the ball case (and others like it) demands much more powerful insight into modal space than is demanded by the proposal that we represent counterfactuals about the direction in which the ball will continue once it is thrown. Perception does not seem to be that powerful.

5.5 RAW FEELS

So far, I've criticized the hypothesis that the phenomenal contrast between the target and the contrasting experience is a difference exclusively in non-causal contents of the visual parts of each experience. I now turn to the hypothesis that there is a special raw feel (i.e., a nonrepresentational phenomenal feature) that is missing from the contrasting experience but not from the target experience. Call this raw feel factor X. Think of X as a raw feel for causation. Experiences with factor X tend to give rise to judgments of causation.

According to the raw-feel hypothesis, when factor X is added to a visual experience with certain non-causal contents, the result is an experience of unity of the sort that is found in the target experiences.[10] Let's call an experience that combines X with a visual experience that has the non-causal contents that occur in the two ball experiences "$X+C$" (C for contents). X is the raw feel that is supposed to be missing from the contrasting experience but present in the target experience in the ball case, and C is the non-causal content that is shared by the visual parts of each experience in the pair.

C is an instance of a specific class of non-causal contents. Let's call such non-causal contents *special* when they are poised to figure in experiences of unity. Non-causal contents are special just in case combining a visual experience having those contents with raw-feel factor X creates an experience of unity. If the raw-feel hypothesis is true, then in the curtain case and in the ball case, all of the visual experiences (i.e., all four of them) have special non-causal contents.

According to the raw-feel hypothesis, the experience of unity is $X+C$. For the proposal to get off the ground, it must be possible to have a visual experience with contents C without X, since X is supposed to be the factor that makes the two ball cases phenomenally different. We can also ask: can X ever occur without special non-causal contents?

---

10. According to a different raw-feel hypothesis, the contrasting experience includes a special raw feel that the target experience doesn't. Here the special raw feel is a kind of phenomenal default. It is a raw feel associated with a lack of unity phenomenology. This proposal seems unmotivated.

This possibility is not obviously coherent. It is doubtful that we can have any grip on what X is, apart from those experiences of some events being unified. Given the role that X is supposed to play in the raw feel hypothesis, any grip on which phenomenal character the putative raw feel X is will come from the examples in which some events seem to be unified. It is at best elusive whether there is a raw feel X that could be abstracted from the cases that the proponent of the raw feel hypothesis has to use to identify it in the first place.

The raw feel hypothesis thus seems most plausible in a form that holds that X can occur only in experiences that have special non-causal contents. But this form of the hypothesis faces a challenge of its own. If X can occur only with special non-causal contents, then its status as a raw feel may be called into question. Compare the discussion of spectrum inversion, where it sometimes seems that one philosopher's quale could be another philosopher's Fregean or (quasi-Fregean) mode of presentation. For instance, suppose that redness can be represented by both phenomenally red and phenomenally green experiences, and that phenomenally red experiences can represent either red, green, or another hue, depending on the properties that normally cause such experiences.[11] And let's suppose that phenomenal redness can occur only in experiential representations of color properties—a substantive assumption to which we shall return in a moment. Is phenomenal redness a quale, or a mode of presentation of color properties? The analogous question about X is this: if factor X can occur only in experiences with special non-causal contents, we can ask: is X really a raw feel, or is it a mode of presentation of some sort of unity? If it is the latter, then X is not, after all, a raw feel that is added on to C, but rather an aspect of content with which an experience represents some kind of unity.

11. Many discussions are based on such assumptions, including Shoemaker (1994, 2000), Byrne and Hilbert (1997), and Chalmers (2004).

We can develop this challenge further. Intuitively, something makes phenomenal redness suitable for accompanying the representation of color properties but unsuitable for accompanying the representation of properties such as motion or solidity. A similar asymmetry is found in X: X is supposed to be especially well suited for accompanying special non-causal contents, rather than representations of greenness. Where do these asymmetries come from? One answer is that phenomenal redness places a constraint on which other contents or representational features an experience will have.[12] When a phenomenal feature can belong only to experiences in which certain properties or certain kinds of properties are represented, then it is playing a role in determining which properties the experience represents. This makes it a kind of a representational feature of experience, rather than a raw feel.[13]

This observation brings into focus a dilemma for the raw-feel hypothesis. If the raw-feel factor X cannot occur without special non-causal contents, then it is a representational feature of experience. If X can occur without C or any other special non-causal contents, then the phenomenal contribution that X is making to the experiences in which it occurs is so elusive as to undermine any reason to believe that there is any such phenomenal factor as X.

Drawing on similar considerations, a second objection can be raised against the raw-feel hypothesis. According to this objection, the raw-feel hypothesis has no satisfactory account of the

12. One kind of Naïve Realism has a different account of the asymmetry: phenomenal redness enables you to see redness but need not enable you to see motion or solidity, because phenomenal redness can occur in an experience only when redness is instantiated and you're in contact with it, so spectrum inversion is not possible. Something like this answer is endorsed by Fish (2009, chap. 1), and also by Langsam (2011). Given the compatibility of Naïve Realism with the Content View, this account of the asymmetry is compatible with the idea that phenomenal redness determines which properties an experience represents.

13. So, in the case of color, if phenomenal redness places constraints on contents of experience, then it is a representational feature, not a quale.

relationship between $X+C$ and non-experiential representations of causation.

We can begin by asking whether it is metaphysically possible for $X+C$ to occur without any representation of causation of any sort—either a non-experiential representation of causation, or a representation of causation in a non-sensory experience. (Naturally, the proponent of the raw-feel hypothesis is committed to disallowing that it can occur with a representation of causation in visual perceptual experience, since the hypothesis is meant to be an alternative to the Causal Thesis.) According to the raw-feel hypothesis, $X+C$ is an experience of unity. So if $X+C$ can occur without any representation of causation, then one can have an experience of unity without judging that the ball's landing in the plant caused the lights to go out, without being disposed to believe (or judge) this, without supposing or being struck by the thought that this causal relation obtains, and without any other kind of representation of causation.

Once representations of causation are entirely divorced from $X+C$, $X+C$ starts to look less plausible as a hypothesis about what the feeling of unity is. We initially identify the feeling of unity by fixing precisely on cases where, in some broad sense, a causal relation seems to obtain. If $X+C$ can be divorced even from such seeming, then it becomes worse as a candidate for the experience of unity that gets the phenomenal contrast off the ground. At best, $X+C$ could represent a non-causal kind of unity. But as we saw earlier, in the ball case there does not seem to be any good candidate for what the kind of unity could be. It seems as if the best version of the raw-feel proposal links $X+C$ to a representation of causation of some sort.

One way to link $X+C$ to a representation of causation develops Hume's idea that our representations of causation arise from a special kind of transition the mind makes between ideas.[14] If $X+C$

14. Hume (1888, I.iii.XIV). In a different interpretation of Hume, the claim that there is such a transition could just be a description of the

is a transition to a representation of causation, then it could not occur in the absence of such a representational state. So $X+C$ would be connected to a representation of causation with metaphysical necessity.

We can then ask: what kind of representation of causation is $X+C$ a transition to? It is either an experiential representation (where the experience is not a visual perceptual experience), or it is a non-experiential representation. I'll argue in the next section that there is no good candidate for an experiential representation distinct from visual perceptual experience. I don't know of a knockdown case against the possibility that it is a non-experiential representation distinct from a doxastic state of some sort. But it is not clear what kind of non-doxastic state this could be. If it is supposed to be a cognitive phenomenally conscious state, then it collapses into the proposal we'll consider next.

5.6 NON-SENSORY EXPERIENCES

Let us consider the idea that in the ball case both visual experiences have the same non-causal contents, but that the target experience includes a non-sensory experience that represents causation, whereas the contrasting experience does not.

We can see right away that the accompanying non-sensory experience will not always be an occurrent judgment, since in the ball case you don't believe that the ball's landing in the plant caused the lights to go off. But perhaps there is some other non-sensory experience for it to be, such as an occurrent state of being "struck" with the thought that the ball caused the lights to go off.

---

psychological structure underlying experience. If so, it is neutral on the Causal Thesis. In focusing on Hume's claim about a transition between mental items, I'm ignoring other commitments about the nature of ideas that Hume may have had that might rule out the Causal Thesis.

Suppose that you have been thinking on and off about what it would be like if you threw a ball, it landed in a plant with a thud, and its so landing caused the lights to go out. Throughout the day, you might be periodically struck by the thought that a certain ball's landing in a plant with a thud caused the lights to go out. On some of these occasions, you're struck by this thought while playing catch with the ball you've been musing about. And on one of those occasions, you're struck with the thought just as the lights really do go out, just after the ball you've been throwing (and musing about) lands with a thud.

All of this could happen without it seeming to you that the ball's landing in the plant was unified in the way we've been discussing with the light's going out. You might be so caught up in your musings that you don't pay much attention to the events of the ball landing in the plant and the lights going out. You see the ball land, and, we can suppose, you have a visual experience with non-causal contents that in quick succession, the ball lands and the lights go out (these are, roughly, the special non-causal contents C). But it seems plain that you could fail to put two and two together. Your visual experience might occur outside the radar of your musing. If so, then being struck with a thought that has causal contents, even if it happens simultaneously with your visual experience, will not suffice to produce the feeling of unity that is distinctive of our target experiences.

One might respond that the relevant occurrent thought to focus on is not a general thought that a specific ball's landing causes the lights to go out, but rather a thought that would be natural to express using demonstrative expressions for specific events, such as "*that* event of the ball's landing caused *that* event of the lights going out," where the demonstratives pick out the events they do at least partly in virtue of your visual experience.[15] But even this kind of thought could be had in the absence of the feeling of unity. All that the demonstrative contents do is ensure that the thoughts

15. For more discussion of perceptual anchoring see Siegel (2002).

are about specific events. You could suppose, imagine, or hypothesize that the events were causally related, without their seeming to be unified at all, let alone causally related. What's needed to make this option plausible is a mode in which to entertain the relevant contents, a mode that is neither a judgment nor a visual experience. Once the events seem causally related, and once they seem that way in an experience, it is hard to say what is preventing the experience from being visual.

I've argued that the Causal Thesis is, on the face of it, a good explanation of the unity experienced in the ball and the curtain cases. The alternatives seem to fall into one of three broad and exhaustive categories: target experiences have distinctive non-causal contents missing in contrasting experiences; target experiences involve a special raw feel that generates the feeling of unity when combined with non-causal contents; or target experiences are accompanied by non-sensory experiences that represent causation. There are doubtless other versions of each option that remain unconsidered. But I have addressed the main challenges facing each alternative: accounting for the relation between occurrent thoughts and visual experiences; the relation between raw feels and contentful states; and the status of unity relations as non-causal.

PART III

OBJECTS

So far, we've been discussing which properties are represented in visual experience by asking which properties figure in the contents of such experience, where contents are a kind of accuracy condition. But we've largely ignored the role of the objects we see in experience. What roles in experiences do these objects play? We can ask more specifically about the role of objects in experiences generally, their role in experiential contents, and their role in phenomenal character. There are four main questions.

Q1*. Are any experiences individuated by the objects we see?

The distinctions we drew in chapter 1 between broad and narrow classes of experience bear on this question. Suppose that you see Franco and he looks sad to you. This state of seeing is individuated in part by Franco. When we ask the same question about phenomenal states, the answer is not settled by any thesis we have defended so far. So our first question is Q1:

Q1. Are any phenomenal states individuated by the objects we see?

The Content View and the Rich Content View are neutral on Q1. Chapter 6 argues that the answer to Q1 is no. The phenomenal state you are in when you see Franco and he looks sad to you is not individuated by Franco. If so, I'll argue, then Naïve Realism (in both its standard and radical forms) is false. However, this conclusion is independent of both the Content View and the Rich Content View, and of our defenses of them.

A second question about the objects we see concerns their role in the contents of experience.

Q2. Are the contents of experience individuated by the objects we see?

Suppose you see Franco and he looks sad to you. Would the experience you have while seeing Franco be accurate with respect to a situation where Franco's twin is sad but Franco isn't, or does the accuracy of the experience depend in every world on whether Franco himself is sad?

The distinction we drew in chapter 2 between strong and weak veridicality bears on Q2. This distinction illuminates how an experience could be both accurate in one way but inaccurate in another with respect to the same world. Let us say that if the accuracy of the experience you have when you see Franco depends in every world on how things are with Franco, then it has accuracy conditions that are singular. Chapter 6 argues that the experience you have when Franco looks sad to you has both singular and non-singular contents. If it does, then the answer to Q2 is: yes and no.

The last two questions concern the role of objects in phenomenal character.

Q3. Does the phenomenal character of hallucinations always differ from the phenomenal character of states of seeing?

Q3 is closely related to Q1. If some phenomenal states are individuated by objects seen, then those states will differ in their character from hallucinations, in which nothing is seen.

Q4 asks about the difference between standard pure visual perceptual experiences and visual experiences traditionally classified as visual sensations, such as having phosphenes or "seeing stars" from being hit on the head:

Q4. How does the phenomenal character of standard visual perceptual experiences differ from the phenomenal character of visual sensations?

Visual sensations are not and do not seem to be perceptions of external, public objects. How can the phenomenological difference between this kind of visual experience and standard visual perceptual experiences best be understood?

Q4 is addressed in chapter 7, which employs the method of phenomenal contrast to make a case that certain perceptual relations between the perceiver and objects she sees (or seems to see) are represented in visual perceptual experiences. So chapter 7 takes us back to the topic of which properties are represented in these experiences. But this time, the focus is on contents that are regularly represented in visual perceptual experience and indeed are distinctive of visual perceptual experiences as a class. The kind of phenomenal contrast at issue in chapter 7 is a general contrast between visual perceptual experiences and visual experience traditionally classified as mere visual sensations. The best explanation of this contrast, I argue, is that these two kinds of visual experiences differ in content.

Addressing these four questions helps fill out a picture of visual experience. If our answers to Q1 and Q4 are right, then perhaps even visual perceptual experiences that include entoptic phenomena are propositional attitudes with some of the same features discussed in connection with the Strong Content View in section 2.6. But regardless of whether phenomenal states have this underlying structure, our answers to Q2 and Q4 bring into focus the general contours of the contents of visual experience. All visual perceptual experiences have nonsingular contents. And all visual perceptual experiences represent K-properties—specifically, the perceptual relations described in chapter 7. Finally, certain states of seeing have singular contents in which these K-properties are attributed to the objects seen, along with all the other properties that those objects look to the perceiver to have. When Franco looks sad to you, you experience him as being sad. Antecedently, this conclusion seems straightforwardly correct. Our answer to Q2 shows how it can be maintained.

Chapter 6

The Role of Objects in Visual Experience

Let us begin with Q2, the question about contents. Suppose you see Franco and he looks sad to you. Would the experience you have while seeing Franco be accurate with respect to a situation where Franco's twin is sad but Franco isn't? Or does the accuracy of the experience depend in every world on whether Franco himself is sad? If its accuracy depends in every world on how things are with Franco, then it has accuracy conditions that are singular.[1]

Prima facie, there is something to be said for both singular and nonsingular accuracy conditions. On the one hand, seeing Franco connects you to him in a way that typically makes it possible for you to form *de re* mental states about him, such as those you might express by saying "That guy needs rest" or "Look how he slumps in his chair."[2] When you see Franco, he looks some way to you,

---

1. More exactly, the contents are singular with respect to Franco, in that they track Franco across worlds. Contents that track times (or places or the perceiver) across worlds would be singular with respect to times (or places or the perceiver). In this chapter, by "singular contents" I'll mean contents that track objects seen across worlds, and by "nonsingular contents" I'll mean contents that do not track these objects across worlds, so the focus here is exclusively on objects seen.

2. Roughly speaking, a belief is *de re* with respect to Franco if it is true of Franco in every world where it is true at all. Contrast the belief that the tallest man in town is tired. This belief may be true of Franco in the world where he is the tallest man in town, while being true of Ray in a world where Franco is wide awake because Ray is the tallest man in town and is tired. So this belief is not *de re* relative to Franco, whereas the beliefs that would be natural to express by saying "Franco is tired" or "He is tired" (while pointing to Franco) are.

and your experience tells you about him. This suggests that your experience has singular accuracy conditions: its accuracy depends on whether Franco has the properties he looks to have—not just on whether anyone has those properties.

On the other hand, there is some force to the idea that the experience of seeing a red cube would be accurate with respect to a world where a qualitatively identical but distinct red cube was at the same location. And if this holds for red cubes, it could hold for people as well. Moreover, it is easy to imagine a hallucination that is indistinguishable from your experience of seeing Franco, from your point of view. Such a hallucination would not connect you to Franco in a way that allowed you to form de re mental states about him, but it could have accuracy conditions nonetheless. For example, there could easily enough be a situation that does not include Franco but is otherwise exactly the way the hallucination presents things as being. This suggests that the hallucination has nonsingular accuracy conditions: it would be accurate with respect to a situation in which Franco's twin or an impostor had exactly the properties that Franco looks to have when you see him, so that its accuracy does not depend in every world on how things are with Franco. If so, then if hallucinations and indistinguishable perceptions have the same contents, the experience you have while seeing Franco has nonsingular accuracy conditions.

The experience you have when Franco looks sad to you cannot be both accurate and inaccurate with respect to the world where Franco isn't sad but his twin is. Yet both singular and nonsingular accuracy conditions seem plausibly associated with experiences. Could these facts be reconciled? They could be, if there were two ways for an experience to be accurate (or inaccurate) with respect to a world. Such a distinction would open up the possibility that with respect to the world where Franco's twin is sad but Franco isn't, the experience you have when Franco looks sad to you is accurate in one way while being inaccurate in another.

One such distinction was drawn in chapter 2. Strongly veridical experiences of a subject are accurate of things the subject sees, whereas weakly veridical experiences are accurate of a situation, if something in the situation has the properties presented in the experience. For example, in principle, hallucinations can be weakly veridical without being strongly veridical, by being accurate of the hallucinator's situation, without being accurate of anything the subject sees—since she doesn't see anything. According to one kind of strong veridicality, your experience of seeing Franco would be strongly veridical only with respect to worlds where Franco is sad. But it might still be weakly veridical with respect to the world where Franco's twin is sad while Franco isn't. In this way, the experience would be strongly falsidical but weakly veridical with respect to one and the same world. With respect to that world, it would be accurate in one way but inaccurate in another.[3]

3. Two-dimensionalist theories of content provide a different way in which your experience could have both singular and nonsingular accuracy conditions. Unlike the distinction between strong and weak veridicality, which applies only to visual experiences, the central distinction for two-dimensionalist is between two ways of evaluating experiences for accuracy relative to a possible situation, yielding two intensions (functions from possibilities to extensions) for each contentful state or utterance. This distinction is crucial for two-dimensionalist theories and there are many ways to develop it, but however it is developed, it cuts across the distinction between strong and weak veridicality.

A two-dimensionalist can accept the distinction between strong and weak veridicality while associating two intensions with each kind of veridicality condition. For example, when applied to the case in which Franco looks red to the perceiver, Chalmers' epistemic two-dimensionalist Fregean theory (2004) will say that the weak veridicality conditions will consist in both a primary intension <there exists an object at center-relative location L with a property that normally causes phenomenal redness>, and a secondary intension <Franco, redness>. The strong veridicality conditions will also consist of two intensions. The weak and strong secondary intensions will be the same, and the strong primary intension will differ from the weak primary intension only in the characterization of the object position: <object causing this experience>, where this is a function from centered worlds with an experience, as well as a subject and time, marked at the center.

In this chapter I rely on the distinction between strong and weak veridicality to make a case that experiences have both singular and nonsingular contents. Section 6.2 discusses the distinction between strong and weak veridicality. Section 6.3 adapts the Argument from Appearing to certain states of seeing, and concludes that these states have contents that are singular stemming from strong veridicality conditions, and contents that are nonsingular (in a sense to be explained) stemming from weak veridicality conditions. Section 6.4 draws on related considerations to argue that some instances of phenomenal states have both singular and nonsingular contents, while other instances have only nonsingular contents.

Like the Content View, these conclusions are defended using premises that leave much about the nature of phenomenal states unsettled, and they remain compatible with a wide range of theories about the nature of phenomenal states. Section 6.5 discusses the relationship between phenomenal states and states of seeing, and section 6.6 concludes that no phenomenal states are identical with any states of seeing. This conclusion takes a step beyond the neutrality of the Content View and the Rich Content View on the nature of phenomenal states. But this departure is not needed to defend our account of the role of objects we see in the contents of experience.

6.1 STRONG AND WEAK VERIDICALITY

In section 6.3 I'm going to argue that certain states of seeing have both singular and nonsingular contents. The case for this conclusion relies on a distinction between strong and weak veridicality, which we can now examine more closely.

The distinction between strong and weak veridicality is defined in terms of seeing. Strongly veridical experiences are experiences that are accurate of an object that the subject sees. When you see

Franco, and Franco looks sad to you, your experience is strongly veridical with respect to a world w just in case Franco is sad in w. More generally:

> A state X of a subject S is strongly veridical with respect to a world w, only if X is or is part of a state of seeing o, X attributes properties F to o, and o is F in w.

Only states of seeing can be strongly veridical. A hallucination could not be.

So far, all we have done is define a kind of accuracy condition. It has yet to be seen whether this accuracy condition correlates with any contents of experiences. An argument that it does is coming in section 6.3.

An experience could be strongly veridical, even though the subject's perceptual contact with the object seen is suboptimal.[4] Suppose that Franco looks sad to you, and that he is sad, but that his looking sad is due to a strange one-off intervention in your perceptual process rather than due to his being sad. You see Franco, but intuitively, your relation of perceptual contact is not optimal. Superstrongly veridical experiences are optimal cases of perceptual contact, and thus superstrong veridicality rules out this kind of veridical illusion, whereas strong veridicality does not.[5]

The right-hand side of this definition gives strong veridicality conditions of such states. These accuracy conditions track the object seen (Franco, in our example) across worlds. We start with a world in which a subject S sees Franco, and the strong veridicality conditions of the experience of seeing him track Franco across worlds.

In the other worlds where the strong veridicality conditions are met—that is, in other worlds where Franco is sad—is Franco

---

4. Compare the case of Simone in section 2.2.
5. On superstrong veridicality, see section 2.1. Strong veridicality allows predicative veridical illusions of the kind described in the text above but rules out objectual veridical illusions. Superstrong veridicality rules out both. On varieties of veridical illusion, see footnote 9 in chapter 2.

always seen? It is not built into the notion of strong veridicality that he is. Whether Franco has to be seen in all the worlds where strong veridicality conditions are met depends on which properties the state of seeing presents him as having. In the next chapter I'll argue that all visual perceptual experiences represent that certain perceptual relations hold between perceivers and objects. If these relations are represented in experience, then any worlds in which strong veridicality conditions of visual perceptual experiences are met will be worlds in which someone stands in these perceptual relations to Franco. But this result does not come along for free as part of a strong veridicality condition.[6]

Let's get back to the distinction between strong and weak veridicality. Whereas an experience can be strongly veridical only if it is or is part of a state of seeing, an experience can be weakly veridical even if it is a hallucination. Weakly veridical experiences are accurate of anything that has the properties presented in the experience. More exactly, as a first pass:

6. Different strong veridicality conditions could be defined that build in the perception of the object across worlds. The first notion below builds this in and is *de re* with respect to the object seen (Franco, in the example), whereas the second notion below builds it in but is not *de re* with respect to the object seen.

S's state of seeing Franco as sad is strongly-perceptually-veridical-1 with respect to world w only if, in w, S sees Franco and Franco is sad.

S's state of seeing Franco as sad is strongly-perceptually-veridical-2 with respect to world w only if, in w, there is an object x that S sees and x is sad.

Strong veridicality is a notion designed to articulate the conditions under which an experience is accurate of a thing seen. The two versions of strong perceptual veridicality are two ways to develop this idea. (Something like the second version could apply to hallucinations:

S's hallucination that there is something with property cluster F is perceptually veridical with respect to w only if, in w, there is an object x that S sees, and x is F.)

Weak veridicality (first pass):
An experience that presents property cluster F is weakly veridical with respect to a world w only if something is F in w.

Any experience that is strongly veridical with respect to a world is also weakly veridical with respect to that world. But the converse does not hold. For one thing, hallucinations can be weakly veridical but not strongly veridical. For another, a state of seeing can be weakly veridical while failing to be veridical of the object seen, as in objectual veridical illusions such as the following. You see a red cube that looks orange, but there is an orange cube hidden behind a mirror at exactly the location where the red cube appears to be located. Here the state of seeing is weakly veridical but not strongly veridical.

The two veridicality conditions just defined (strong and weak veridicality) are both only-if conditions. They can be turned into iff conditions that are potentially suitable for being experience contents by making additional assumptions about the role of properties in the contents of experience. Russellian theories will allow that the only-if conditions can be turned into iff conditions as they stand. Fregean and centered-worlds accounts can each adjust the conditions to yield iff conditions. For instance, Fregean accounts can get iff conditions by adjusting the right-hand side to incorporate modes of presentation. A centered-world account would replace reference to properties with centering features, and worlds with centered worlds, to get an iff condition.[7]

One might think that the first-pass definition of weak veridicality has to be adjusted using centered worlds to a get a veridicality

---

7. For discussion, see section 2.4. A Fregean version of strong veridicality might look like this:

A state X of a subject S is strongly veridical with respect to a world w iff X is a state of seeing an object o, X attributes properties F to o, and something in w has a cluster of properties that meet the conditions on extension that F meets in the world where S has X.

condition that accords with some simple intuitions about veridicality. Suppose you see a cube that looks red and cubical. For
your experience to be weakly veridical with respect to a world, it
is not enough that there is a red cube anywhere in the world.
Some sort of location feature must be included in the veridicality
condition, or else it will be too easy to be weakly veridical. In the
case of hallucination, one might think, the only locations that can
be represented are locations relative to the subject, and for these
to figure in veridicality conditions, something like centered
worlds is needed. Even in non-hallucinatory experiences, locations of things seem to be presented as locations relative to the
subject. If so, then a better definition of weak veridicality is a second pass:

Weak veridicality (second pass):
An experience that presents a cluster of (center-relative) features F
is weakly veridical with respect to a (centered) world w only if
something has features F in w.

For instance, according to the second pass, an experience that presents something as red and cubical and nearby is weakly veridical
with respect to a centered world w only if there is a red cube
nearby the subject at the center of w. In what follows, I will talk
about weak veridicality conditions without making these adjust-
ments, but they should be taken as understood.

We started by noting that prima facie, both singular and nonsingular contents seem plausible to associate with experiences.
With the notions of strong and weak veridicality on the table, we
can see that when you see Franco being sad, your experience
could have both singular and nonsingular contents if singular
contents are strong veridicality conditions while nonsingular contents are weak veridicality conditions. That leaves us with two
questions: First, are either strong veridicality conditions or weak
veridicality conditions contents? Second, are these contents singular or nonsingular?

6.2 THE CONTENTS OF STATES OF SEEING

Suppose you see Franco being sad: he looks sad to you and he is sad. I'll call this state of seeing *seeing Franco being sad*. More generally, when you see an object o, your experience attributes F-ness to o, and o is F, then you are seeing o being F. In section 6.1, we defined strong veridicality conditions for states of seeing, such as the state of seeing Franco being sad. In this section I will argue that these veridicality conditions are singular contents of states of object-seeing that specify how the objects look, such as seeing Franco being sad, and seeing Franco when he looks sad but isn't.

We can distinguish between two kinds of singular contents. In general, for any content that is singular with respect to Franco, whether that content is true in an arbitrary world w depends on how things are with Franco in w. Consider the Russellian contents (a) and (b) below:

(a) <Franco, sadness>
(b) <Ray, being identical with Franco>

Both content (a) and content (b) are singular with respect to Franco. Whether (a) is true in an arbitrary world w depends on whether Franco is sad in w. Whether content (b) is true in w depends on whether Franco is identical with Ray in w. In this way, both contents depend for their truth in w on how things are with Franco in w.

The important contrast between contents (a) and (b) is that Franco figures in a property that is attributed to an object (Ray) in content (b), whereas he is the thing to which a property (sadness) is attributed in the content (a). This contrast helps us draw a distinction among experiences with contents that are singular with respect to Franco. Any state of seeing with the content (a) could anchor a *de re* mental state to Franco, in the sense that it makes Franco available so that the subject can go on to form other *de re* mental states about him. In contrast, suppose you see Ray when

he is so convincingly disguised as Franco that the phenomenal
state you are in is identical to the phenomenal state you are in
when you see Franco and recognize him (whether this is possible
will be discussed shortly). In such a case, your state of seeing
might have the content (b). But even though its content is singular
with respect to Franco, the state of seeing would not anchor any *de
re* mental states to Franco. For instance, if you relied on your state
of seeing to anchor the use of a demonstrative in uttering "Look,
that's Franco!", you would end up referring to Ray rather than to
Franco by your use of "that." If Franco figures predicatively but
not objectually in the content of an experience, then you need not
be seeing him.

Let us call contents of states of seeing that are singular with
respect to an object *o* by virtue of *o*'s being seen "objectually singular contents." And let us call contents of states of seeing that are
singular with respect to an object *o* by virtue of *o*'s figuring in a
property attributed to the object seen "predicatively singular contents." If you see Franco and the properties he looks to have included the property of being identical with Franco, then the contents
of your state of seeing would be both objectually and predicatively
singular with respect to Franco. If a state of seeing had content (b),
it would be objectually singular with respect to Ray, and predicatively but not objectually singular with respect to Franco.

Could the content of an experience be predicatively singular
with respect to Franco, even if you were not seeing him? Suppose
there were a hallucination of Franco being sad, so that something
made it the case that it was a hallucination of Franco and not Franco's twin. Such a hallucination would be predicatively singular
with respect to Franco, since it would be part of the hallucination
that the hallucinated figure was Franco. Could the contents of
such a hallucination be objectually singular with respect to Franco
as well?

The constraints on contents of experiences suggest that a hallucination could not have objectually singular contents. Even a veridical
hallucination could not reliably guide actions or movements with

respect to Franco.[8] Even if, by an amazing coincidence, Franco were present and were located exactly where the hallucination presented him as being, the hallucination could not make it the case that a *de re* belief that Franco is sad is a belief about Franco. While such a hallucination could occur only if the subject had previously been in the kind of contact with Franco that enables *de re* mental states, it does not itself provide any such anchor to Franco.

No experiences that have objectually singular contents will be hallucinations. I will now argue that certain states of seeing have contents that are objectually singular with respect to objects that are seen. The argument adapts the line of reasoning found in the Argument from Appearing (2.4) to states of seeing objects having properties.

The Argument from Seeing

Premise (i*)
All states of seeing objects having properties present clusters of properties as being instantiated by the objects seen.

Premise (ii)
If a state E of seeing object o having properties F presents a cluster of properties F as being instantiated, then:
Necessarily: things are the way E presents them only if property-cluster F is instantiated.

Premise (iii)
If necessarily: things are the way E presents them only if property-cluster F is instantiated, then:
E has a set of accuracy conditions C, conveyed to the subject of E, such that:
C is satisfied in a world only if there is something that has F in that world.

8. If in all the nearby worlds where the putatively hallucinating subject has a phenomenally indistinguishable experience, Franco were present, that would call into question the status of the experience as a hallucination. For discussion, see Lewis (1980) and McLaughlin (1996).

Premise (iv)
If E has a set of accuracy conditions C, conveyed to the subject of
E, such that E is accurate only if C, then:
    E has a set of accuracy conditions C^*, conveyed to the subject of
    E, such that E is accurate iff C^*.

Conclusion: All states of seeing objects having properties have
contents.

The defenses of the original premises (i)–(iv) apply to the variants
in the Argument from Seeing as well. The defense of the original (i)
made a case that properties are presented in experience. In cases of
seeing Franco being sad, these are properties that Franco looks to
you to have. When you see Franco being sad, he looks to you to
have certain properties. This platitude is restated by premise (i*).

In fact, the defense of the original premise (i) supports a stronger
claim than (i*). Premise (i*) is about states of seeing o being F, such
as the state of seeing Franco being sad. When a subject S sees Franco
being sad, Franco is sad. But even if Franco isn't sad, if he nonetheless looks sad when S sees him, then S will be in a state of seeing
that presents Franco as having certain properties, including sadness. The rest of the premises are the same as they are in the original Argument from Appearing, except here E is a state of seeing
(more exactly, a state of seeing an object having certain properties),
instead of a phenomenal state. But the defenses of the premises can
remain the same. In fact, the defense of premise (iv) goes through
more easily, because the complication about objects does not arise.

We can illustrate the reasoning in the Argument from Seeing
with an example. Suppose you see Franco and he looks sad. If this
state is accurate with respect to a world, then the world is the way
the experience presents it as being. The state of seeing Franco
when he looks sad presents Franco as being sad. So for a world to
be the way the state of seeing presents it, Franco must be sad. The
state of seeing Franco being sad thus has objectually singular
accuracy conditions. Such states of seeing are accurate with
respect to a world w, only if Franco is sad in w.

So far, we can conclude that experiences have singular contents. More exactly, states of seeing have objectually singular contents. This conclusion vindicates the idea that experiences play certain special roles vis à vis *de re* mental states by providing relations to particular objects and by attributing properties to them. For example, experiences make it possible for us to form *de re* mental states about the objects we see, and experiences provide evidence for beliefs about those particular objects. The fact that experiences have objectually singular contents may help explain how they play these roles.

We have been discussing states of seeing objects having properties, and states of seeing in which objects look to have properties they lack. One might think that only phenomenal states have weak veridicality conditions, whereas states of seeing objects having properties (or states of seeing objects when they merely look to have certain properties) do not. But so long as these states of seeing have veridicality conditions at all, they have both weak veridicality conditions and strong veridicality conditions. Their weak veridicality conditions are met in any world in which the properties presented in the experience are instantiated. For instance, the weak veridicality conditions of the state of seeing Franco being sad (and the state of seeing Franco when he looks sad but isn't) are satisfied in any world where someone has all the properties that Franco looks to have when he looks sad.

Why think that the weak veridicality conditions of these states of seeing are contents? One reason is that plenty of accuracy conditions are contents, and these include accuracy conditions involving relative locations of the sort that are built into the definition of weak veridicality (on the second pass). In addition, a state of seeing that conveys that Franco is sad also conveys that someone is sad. Suppose you want to know whether there was anyone sad in the room. You look in the room and see Franco, looking melancholic and slumped in his chair. It is hard to imagine an experience that failed to convey that a sad person was in the room while succeeding in conveying that Franco is in the room and sad. The existential generalization of any objectually singular content is available to guide action and seems just as natural to believe as the singular content of which it is a generalization.

Predicative Singularity

The position that experiences can have both singular and non-singular contents respects the possibility that an experience could be both accurate and inaccurate with respect to the same world. For instance, there is some prima facie plausibility, we suggested, to the idea that the state of seeing Franco being sad might be strongly falsidical but weakly veridical with respect to the world where Franco's twin is sad but Franco isn't.

However, by itself, the thesis that the state of seeing Franco being sad has objectually nonsingular contents does not secure the result that this state of seeing is weakly veridical with respect to the world where Franco's twin is sad but Franco isn't. When Franco looks sad to you, if he also looks to have some properties that no one else could have, then there won't be any world in which Franco's twin has those very properties. A fortiori, there won't be any such world with respect to which your state of seeing is weakly veridical. To get the result that there are worlds with respect to which states of seeing are weakly veridical but strongly falsidical, what's needed is an additional assumption that it is possible for someone other than Franco to have all the properties that Franco looks to have when you see him. This possibility could be blocked by a form of predicative singularity.

In chapter 4 we discussed the idea that trees can look different to you before and after you learn that they are pine trees. The same thing might happen with Franco. He might look different to you after you have gotten to know him, compared to when you first met.[9]

9. Cf. Siewert (1998, 257–58): "Think of how individual people look different to you after you have gotten to know them than they did when you first met." Cf. Fleming (1957, 161).

In the case of pine trees, we argued that the phenomenal contrast was best explained by a change in the contents of experience. Prima facie, the considerations offered for the case of pine trees also support the idea that there is some change in the contents of experience before and after you recognize a person. There need not be any difference in non-K properties represented, or even in focal attention (you might be staring hard at the face trying to remember who this person is, when suddenly it dawns on you that it's Franco). The property of being familiar to you does not correlate with a feeling of recognizing Franco, since he might look familiar to you before you realize who he is. There need not always be a constant stream of occurrent cognitive states representing that the person you see is Franco; and as in the case of pine trees, it's hard to see what kind of background phenomenology could be at work (see section 4.2). If parallel considerations apply to the case of person recognition, that opens the possibility that when you recognize Franco, the cluster of properties that he looks to have when you see him includes the property of being Franco.

Assuming that the phenomenal contrast is best explained by a change in the contents of the state of seeing Franco being sad, there are several ways in which contents could change with recognition. Not all of them result in predicatively singular contents. These responses mirror responses to Frege's puzzle of identity. For instance, according to a proposal along the lines of metalinguistic responses to the puzzle, when you see Franco and recognize him, your state of seeing represents that Franco is the subject of a dossier about Franco, where the dossier could be about other people in other worlds.[10] According to a descriptivist Fregean proposal, when you see Franco and recognize him, your state of

---

10. An individual could be the subject of a dossier without satisfying all of the information contained in it. For discussion of this idea, see Perry (1980) and Dickie (2011).

seeing represents that he has a cluster of properties constituting a mode of presentation that could pick out Franco in one world, but other people in other worlds. Neither of these proposals would make the contents of the state of seeing Franco predicatively singular.[11]

In contrast, predicative singularity results if your state of seeing Franco when you recognize him represents the property of being Franco, without representing it under a mode of presentation that could denote anyone else. It remains unclear, however, how this proposal responds to Frege's puzzle, or how it reflects the phenomenal change that can be brought about by recognizing Franco.[12]

11. Chalmers's two-dimensionalist Fregean response to this phenomenon avoids predicative singularity at the level of primary intension while embracing it at the other level of content. According to this theory, when you see Franco and recognize him, your state of seeing might represent the property of being identical with Franco under a mode of presentation that picks out Franco in the world where you see him but could pick out other people in other worlds. Here the mode of presentation generates predicatively nonsingular contents, while at the level of reference the contents are predicatively singular. This result leads to a mixed verdict on the accuracy of the experience in which you recognize Franco and he looks sad, with respect to the world where Franco's twin is sad but Franco isn't. At the level of the primary intension, predicative singularity is avoided and weak veridicality conditions are satisfied. At the level of the secondary intension, the weak veridicality conditions are not satisfied and predicative singularity is embraced.

However, weak secondary intensions (like strong secondary intensions) are already objectually singular, and so inaccurate with the respect to the world where Franco's twin is sad but Franco isn't. We began with the idea that there are worlds with respect to which an experience of seeing Franco being sad is both accurate and inaccurate, and the two-dimensionalist preserves this idea in their own way, independently of any considerations about recognition.

12. Day after day, you encounter your kitchen table, your winter coat, your best friend's shoes, etc. Even if recognizing people and places can make a phenomenal impact, going with predicative singularity we should expect a different kind of effect on contents in the case of recognizing artifacts. Though we could, we typically don't name even those

Whichever response to the phenomenology of recognizing particular people turns out to be correct, we can conclude that states of seeing have objectually singular contents correlated with strong veridicality conditions, and objectually nonsingular contents correlated with weak veridicality conditions. Whether these two kinds of accuracy conditions are satisfied in different worlds depends on whether the contents are predicatively singular.

Because states of seeing are not necessarily individuated by their phenomenal character, our conclusions about their contents tell us little about the nature of phenomenal states, or about their role in states of seeing. Just as the Argument from Appearing concludes that all phenomenal states have contents while leaving open what structure phenomenal states have, the Argument from Seeing concludes that all states of seeing in which an object o looks F have objectually singular contents while leaving open what structure those states have. For all that has been argued so far, states of seeing may be complex states, structured by a phenomenal

---

artifacts we regularly use and re-identify, such as our butter dishes, pajamas, refrigerators, and so on. By and large we seem to reserve proper names for people and places, leaving ourselves without linguistic labels that track artifacts across worlds. (Perhaps in the same vein, the sense of unease that most people feel at the prospect of tele-transportation is much weaker when it involves the replacement of a butter dish with a duplicate, compared with the replacement of oneself or one's best friend.) Since we find this discrepancy between linguistic and conceptual representations of artifacts on the one hand and people (and places) on the other, it seems reasonable to expect to find it in experience contents as well. And if we do, then there will be significant limits on the cases of predicative singularity in experience, even if the best account of the effect of recognizing people on the contents of experience makes those contents predicatively singular. If recognizing artifacts makes an impact on the contents of experience, the contents will likely involve properties that can be shared, such as the property of being a coat worn regularly by your best friend, or of being a butter dish that was on the table yesterday. This kind of content does not lead to predicative singularity.

state that is appropriately related to external facts, or they may be identical with phenomenal states. In section 6.4, we will examine further the relationship between phenomenal states and states of seeing. For now, we can just ask whether phenomenal states have contents that are singular, nonsingular, or both.

6.3 THE CONTENTS OF PHENOMENAL STATES

Some hallucinations present the subject with properties that seem to be instantiated by things such as daggers and people slumped in chairs. These hallucinations are visual perceptual experiences. We argued in section 6.2 that such hallucinations do not have objectually singular contents. Given the Content View, according to which all visual perceptual experiences have contents, it follows that hallucinations have objectually nonsingular contents. More exactly, the token phenomenal states that figure in hallucinations have objectually nonsingular contents.[13]

What about the phenomenal states that figure in states of seeing? If there are phenomenal states that are identical with the states of seeing discussed in the previous section, then our conclusions about those states of seeing will carry over to these phenomenal states as well, with the result that such phenomenal states have both objectually singular and objectually nonsingular contents. And a case can be made that the token phenomenal states that figure in token states of seeing have objectually singular contents, even if no phenomenal types are identical with states of seeing.

According to premise (i*) of the Argument from Seeing, the state of seeing Franco being sad presents Franco as sad. Without being in

---

13. Are there phenomenal types that are specific to hallucination? I argue against this thesis in section 6.6. But the Content View together with the thesis that hallucinations lack objectually singular contents entails that such phenomenal types, if they exist, have objectually nonsingular contents.

some visual phenomenal state, Franco would not look any way at all. Let us fix on a specific occasion on which you see Franco being sad, and let P be the phenomenal state you're in when you see Franco on that occasion. So on that occasion, you instantiate P. The instance of P plays an indispensable role in presenting Franco as sad. If P covaries with a specific profile of properties, then there is a clear sense in which the instance of P presents Franco as having those properties. Even if P could figure in states of seeing that present different properties to Franco on different occasions (e.g., red in one case, green in another), this does not detract from the role of the instance of P in presenting the properties that Franco looks to have each time. This is because there is no non-phenomenal part of the token state of seeing besides the instance of P that could play this role. If the instance of P presents Franco as having certain properties, then by the reasoning in the rest of the Argument from Seeing, this token phenomenal state has objectually singular contents.

Do these token phenomenal states have objectually nonsingular contents as well? Earlier, we argued that states of seeing have non-objectually singular contents, given the plausibility of the thesis that the weak veridicality conditions of states of seeing are conveyed to the subject. The same considerations apply equally well here. Just as the phenomenal states convey that Franco is sad, they also convey that someone is sad. If so, then the token phenomenal states that figure in states of seeing have both objectually singular and objectually nonsingular contents.

I've argued that the token phenomenal states in hallucinations have exclusively nonsingular contents, while other token phenomenal states in certain states of seeing (such as seeing Franco when he looks sad) have both objectually singular and objectually nonsingular contents. In defending these conclusions, it has not been necessary to rely on theses about the underlying nature of phenomenal states, such as theses that take a stand on whether any of them are identical with states of seeing. What we can take for granted so far is that experiences present the subject with properties in a way that generates both (objectually) singular and nonsingular contents. But are these properties ever presented in phenomenal states that are identical with states of seeing? This leads us from the question about the role of objects in the contents of experience (Q2) to a question about their role in phenomenal states (Q1).

6.4 PHENOMENAL STATES: INTERNALISM VERSUS PURE DISJUNCTIVISM

Suppose once again that you are seeing Franco being sad. As before, P is the phenomenal character had by your state of seeing Franco being sad. What sort of property is P? We can distinguish between three main positions, which can be illustrated using our exemplary phenomenal state P.

First, according to pure disjunctivist positions, P is identical with the state of seeing Franco being sad and so cannot be shared by that state and a hallucination. The other two positions hold that P (which you have when you see Franco being sad) could be had even if you were hallucinating. I'll call these positions internalist. According to pure internalism, P is neither a disjunctive property nor a property that can be realized by any states of seeing. According to disjunctive internalism, P is either a disjunctive property that has a state of seeing as one of its disjuncts, or a property that can be realized by a more fundamental state of seeing, as well as by a hallucination. Here "realization" is something like the relation that holds between the property of playing a certain role, and a state that plays that role. We'll see some examples shortly.

These positions give us three different answers to Q1: Are any phenomenal states individuated by the objects we see? If pure disjunctivism is true, then the answer is yes: the phenomenal states that are identical with states of seeing are individuated by the objects we see. If pure internalism is true, then the answer is no: no phenomenal states are individuated by the objects we see. If disjunctive internalism is true, then the answer is no, with a qualification: no phenomenal states are individuated by the objects we see, but the objects we see may individuate some disjuncts of phenomenal states, or some realizations of them. In section 6.5 I'll argue that the answer to Q1 is no.

Let us consider some examples of each position.

Pure Internalism There are many examples of pure internalism. Consistently with pure internalism, phenomenal states could consist in "directly" perceiving mental items such as sense-data, in raw feels, in a propositional attitude with nonsingular contents, or in some combination.

Pure Disjunctivism Consider standard Naïve Realism, which takes a certain class of non-hallucinatory experiences to be perceptual relations to an object and some of its properties. Earlier (in section 2.5), we called this the class of Good experiences, where different versions of standard Naïve Realism may define the class of Good experiences differently.[14]

There is reason to consider standard Naïve Realism a form of pure disjunctivism. On any version of standard Naïve Realism, Good experiences will presumably include superstrongly veridical ones. Now, it is trivially true that when one has a superstrongly veridical experience, one stands in a perceptual relation to an object and some of its properties. If Naïve Realism were the thesis that superstrongly veridical experiences were perceptual relations to objects and some of their properties, it too would be trivially true. What's needed is a way to formulate standard Naïve Realism that makes it a substantive thesis about superstrongly veridical experiences.

---

14. E.g., illusions may be included or not (cf. Byrne and Logue's distinction in (2008) between VI versus H disjunctivism, and V versus IH disjunctivism), and Good experiences may be merely strongly veridical or restricted to the superstrongly veridical.

One way to do this is to make Naïve Realism a thesis about the visual phenomenal state one is in when one has Good experiences.[15] Naïve Realism so construed is a form of pure disjunctivism. According to this version of pure disjunctivism, phenomenal character P is the property of seeing Franco being sad. This property is a perceptual relation with the subject at one end, and Franco and his sadness at the other end, where the complex of Franco and sadness is not the kind of thing that can be true or false. For instance, it might be a concrete state of affairs consisting of Franco and his sadness. Such perceptual relations are not instantiated in the corresponding hallucination, or in cases where you see Franco's twin looking sad but don't see Franco. So, according to Naïve Realism, these experiences differ phenomenally from your experience when you see Franco looking sad.

This construal of Naïve Realism gives us a first pure disjunctivist theory, and we can distinguish it from a second and a third pure disjunctivist theory. The second pure disjunctivist theory identifies P with the state of seeing that Franco is sad. According to this view, P is a perceptual relation between the subject on the one hand and Franco and his sadness on the other, where the latter relatum is a true proposition. This state of seeing is a factive state.

According to this theory, when you see Franco and his sadness, the phenomenal character of your experience consists in the state of seeing Franco being sad. It shares this feature with standard Naïve Realism. These two theories are substantive proposals about the nature of phenomenal character, but they construe the state of seeing differently. The first theory construes this state as a

15. Campbell (2002, 116) takes this approach. In contrast, Martin (2004, 2006), formulates Naïve Realism by saying that being a Good experience is the fundamental kind to which such experiences belong. Neither approach alters the dialectic surrounding Naïve Realism and the Content View in chapter 2. Standard versions of Naïve Realism construed in either way still entail the Content View, and radical versions of it are still incompatible with the Content View.

relation to something that cannot be true or false, whereas the second construes it as a factive attitude toward a true proposition. According to a third pure disjunctivist theory, P is the nonfactive state of seeing Franco when he looks sad. Unlike the state of seeing Franco being sad, this state can be shared between states of seeing Franco being sad and the state of seeing Franco when he looks sad but isn't.

It is also possible to formulate pure disjunctivism (in any of these three forms) in such a way that P can be shared between states of seeing different objects that are or appear to be qualitatively identical, but cannot be shared with any hallucination. For instance, instead of identifying P with the state of seeing Franco being sad, this variant of pure disjunctivism would identify P with the state of seeing an object being sad, or with the state of seeing an object looking sad. Here, P could be shared between the state of seeing Franco being sad and the state of seeing Franco's twin being sad, but it couldn't be shared by any hallucination.

Disjunctive Internalism Although disjunctive internalism does not identify P with any state of seeing Franco, such as the state of seeing Franco being sad, or the state of seeing him when he looks sad, it may well hold that P is multiply realized by these states.[16]

The simplest version of disjunctive internalism identifies P with a disjunction of the state of seeing Franco being sad and with intuitively "matching" states, without purporting to characterize P independently of these disjuncts. The main motivation for this view is the idea that states of seeing are in some way more fundamental than phenomenal properties that can be shared with hallucinations, and so phenomenal properties should be defined in terms of states of seeing.

---

16. The disjunctivist internalist's construal of P thus may not be disjunctive properties in Fodor's sense (1997), since he reserves "disjunctive property" for properties that are not nomic and not projectible, in contrast with multiply realized properties, which are. Phenomenal properties as the disjunctivist internalist construes them may well be projectible.

Some positions that are advertised as disjunctivist, such as Martin (2004, 2006), can be seen as this form of disjunctive internalism. Though he does not present it this way, Martin's version of disjunctivism can be thought of as the view that P is a disjunctive property, with the state of seeing Franco being sad as one disjunct and the property of being indiscriminable from this state as the other. Hallucinations and illusions consist in the indiscriminability property, whereas Good experiences consist in states of seeing Franco being sad.[17] Martin's view can be thought of as combining disjunctivism about phenomenal states with internalism about perceptual experience. According to him, perceptual experiences are all and only states with indiscriminabilty properties.[18]

A second kind of disjunctive internalism could identify P with the property of being indiscriminable from a state of seeing Franco being sad. Then P could be realized by the state of seeing Franco when he looks sad, the state of seeing Franco's twin when he looks sad, and perhaps hallucinations that "match" these experiences. (We will discuss indiscriminability properties further momentarily.) Here, too, the phenomenal property is defined in terms of states of seeing.

Thirdly, disjunctive internalism could construe P as a state that can be realized by different relations of awareness of properties. According to Johnston (2004), in hallucinations and illusions the subject is aware of uninstantiated universals, whereas in a superstrongly veridical experience with the same phenomenal character,

---

17. All three kinds of state share the indiscriminability property, but that property has a different status in Good experiences than it has in the other experiences, because it is the fundamental kind to which the other experiences belong, whereas it is not the fundamental kind to which Good experiences belong.

18. For example, "the concept of perceptual experience in general is that of situations indiscriminable from veridical perception" (Martin 2004, 56).

she is aware of instances of those same properties.[19] For instance, a hallucinating subject might be aware of the uninstantiated universals redness and cubicality, where the perceiver would be aware of a particular cube's redness and cubicality. In a simplified example, redness and cubicality provide a basis for determining which hallucinations and states of seeing belong to the same phenomenal property.

6.5 WHY INTERNALISM?

The mass production of silverware makes it easy to assemble matching table settings. If mass production goes as it should, then any two forks from the fork machine could be combined with any two knives to yield two matching sets of silverware. This uniformity simplifies the task of setting a table with uniform places. No matter which forks you select, they will look the same. When you see one of the forks beside your plate, it is easy to imagine a situation in which a different fork from the set is in exactly the same position, and in which the table setting looks exactly the same way to you. It is also easy to imagine a hallucination of a table setting just like the one you are seeing. And if there is (or if there could be) a table setting that looks exactly the same way to you even with different forks, and if there could be a hallucination of exactly the same scene, this would suggest that the phenomenal states in all of these situations could be exactly the same. Internalism about phenomenal states is motivated by the idea that there need be no phenomenal differences between the states of seeing

19. In Johnston (2004) the properties in the sensible profile are universals, but Johnston (2006) emphasizes that in superstrongly veridical experiences, one enjoys contact with "exemplifications of properties by objects and quantities of stuff (the snubnosedness of Socrates, or the astringency of the calvados)," which seem closer to tropes than universals.

two qualitatively identical table settings, or between these and a hallucination of just such a table setting.

Whether or not internalism is true, there are clearly pairs of perceptions (such as the states of seeing either of the forks next to your plate) and hallucinations that seem the same from the subject's point of view. Some properties beyond the properties of seeing and hallucinating are needed to explain what it is for certain hallucinations and states of seeing to "match," such as a hallucination of Franco sitting down, and a state of seeing Franco sitting down. Internalism about phenomenal character provides an account of what these pairs of experiences have in common.

Pure disjunctivists also need a way to account for the fact that certain hallucinations and states of seeing are naturally grouped together. Even if such experiences are not phenomenally the same, by the lights of pure disjunctivism, they will be phenomenally more similar to one another than any of them is to the state of seeing nothing but an undifferentiated red expanse that looks red (we assume that nothing in the scene when you see Franco being sad looks red). Internalism can easily account for this phenomenal similarity: by its lights, the experiences share phenomenal properties. Pure disjunctivism, in contrast, cannot easily account for the respects in which all matching experiences are phenomenally similar. We can see this by considering the significant obstacles that stand in the way of the strategies that are available to them.

A pure disjunctivist might suggest that matching experiences are similar with respect to property instances that are perceived— such as the instances of properties shared by matching forks. But in cases of hallucination, no such properties will be instantiated, so no instances of these properties will be perceived.

A related suggestion is that matching experiences are phenomenally similar with respect to the properties that are presented in each experience in the following way: in hallucinations and illusions, the subject S is aware of the same properties whose instances S is aware of in superstrongly veridical experiences, as in Johnston's view. So subjects are aware of ontologically different things in hallucinations or illusions on the one hand and super-strongly veridical experiences on the other. In cases of hallucina-tion and illusion, the subject is aware of properties on their own, without being aware of any instances of those properties. But matching experiences are phenomenally similar with respect to the properties that figure in each kind of object of awareness.

Since according to this position, the same properties are pre-sented to the subject in all matching experiences, it is hard to see why such awareness would be missing from the superstrongly veridical case. If the subject is aware of the same properties on their own in all matching experiences, then there is a state of prop-erty awareness that is sufficient for being in P, putting it at odds with pure disjunctivism.

A different suggestion is that matching experiences are similar with respect to their functional role in the subject's mental life. The functional role would have to be narrow, rather than wide, since a wide functional role would include inputs from external objects that are seen, and *de re* mental states about such objects that the subject could go on to form. Assuming that such a narrow functional role could be defined, it seems possible in principle for a creature to be so configured that a phenomenally dissimilar state (such as the state of seeing an undifferentiated red expanse that looks red) could play the same functional role. If so, then no narrow functional role will mark the respects in which the state of seeing Franco being sad and all matching experiences are phe-nomenally more similar to one another than they are to a halluci-nation of a uniform red expanse.

In accounting for the phenomenal similarity between matching experiences, probably the most powerful strategy for the pure dis-junctivist is to invoke an epistemic property of experiences, such as the property of being indiscriminable by introspection from a state of seeing. According to the versions of disjunctivism that have addressed this question in most detail, the relevant pairs of experiences have in common the merely epistemic property of being indiscriminable from a certain kind of veridical perception.

For instance, the strongly veridical experience of seeing Franco sitting down (i.e., the state of seeing Franco sitting down) is indiscriminable from itself, and certain hallucinations share this indiscriminability property. The most developed discussion of indiscriminability properties is that of Martin (2004, 2006), who draws on Williamson's notion of indiscriminability. As Martin employs the notion, if an experience is indiscriminable from a veridical perception of a red cube as such, then it's not possible to know on the basis of introspection alone that the experience is not a veridical perception of a red cube as such.

There are at least two objections to the idea that matching experiences can be identified by the properties of being indiscriminable from specific veridical perceptions.[20] First, consider an experience of seeing a virtual-reality scene made to look just like what is depicted in Escher's drawing of the impossible staircase. There seem to be no veridical perceptions from which seeing such a scene would be indiscriminable. Yet, there could be a hallucination of an impossible staircase that "matched" a case of seeing the virtual-reality scene.[21]

Second, the notion of indiscriminability employed by disjunctivists is a cognitive notion and thus seems inapplicable to creatures who lack certain cognitive resources but who can nonetheless have experiences. Consider a creature who is too cognitively unsophisticated to be able to form judgments. There won't be any pair of experiences such that the creature can know that they are distinct from one another—since the creature can't know anything at all. So, the disjunctivist's proposal to use shared specific

20. Both objections are developed in more detail in Siegel (2004), so their treatment of them here is brief.
21. In reply, Martin (2008) suggests dividing the experiences in which one seems to see an impossible scene into local parts that are indiscriminable from veridical perceptions. Even if the experience can be divided into local parts, each of which is indiscriminable from a veridical perception, it remains the case that the experience taken as a whole is not so indiscriminable.

indiscriminability properties (such as the property of being indiscriminable from a veridical perception of a red cube as such) to identify matching pairs of experiences seems unable to identify pairs of matching experiences in cognitively unsophisticated creatures.[22] In short, some way of identifying matching pairs of experiences is needed, and identifying pairs by appealing to indiscriminability properties ultimately may not work.[23]

These considerations about how matching may be understood have several implications.

First, they cast doubt on pure disjunctivism, and on versions of disjunctive internalism that identify phenomenal properties with indiscriminability properties that can be realized by states of seeing. Pure disjunctivists need an account of how hallucinatory and non-hallucinatory experiences can match at all, given that they are supposed to be phenomenally distinct. Disjunctive internalism needs an account of why certain hallucinatory and non-hallucinatory experiences belong to the same phenomenal state. It turns out to be difficult to meet these needs by appealing to indiscriminability properties.

The considerations about indiscriminability also undermine the idea that pure disjunctivism is less of a departure from ordinary thought and talk about perception than pure internalism is— an idea that has been invoked to support the claim that pure disjunctivism should be a default position. Ordinary English has words for seeing and hallucinating, but it does not have words

22. In reply to these objections, Martin (2006) and Fish (2009) invoke the notion of impersonal indiscriminability. For further objections to the disjunctivist's appeal to indiscriminability properties and their notion of impersonal indiscriminability, see Siegel (2008).

23. A different argument that disjunctivism is the default view, given by Martin (2004), focuses on the idea that denying disjunctivism incurs weighty epistemological commitments about the mind. This argument is too intricate to do it justice in this brief space, but it is reconstructed and criticized in Siegel (2004). See also Byrne and Logue (2008) and Soteriou (2009).

that denote phenomenal states that are only contingently states of seeing.[24] If the appeal to indiscriminability properties to identify pairs of matching experiences were entirely anodyne, then pure disjunctivism could be formulated using only conceptual ingredients that we already have, avoiding entirely the idea that phenomenal states are involved in states of seeing but only contingently so. The same could not be said for internalism. What we can now see is that the claim that indiscriminability properties can play the role that pure disjunctivists might try to assign to them embodies substantive claims about the nature of introspective access to mental states. It is thus not an innocuous accompaniment to the idea that some phenomenal states are essentially cases of seeing.

These considerations favoring internalism are not conclusive.[25] But appreciating the irrelevance of internalism about phenomenal states to the central questions about the contents of experience is more important than establishing its truth.

24. Following Hinton (1973) and Byrne and Logue (2008), note that the word "experience" as used outside philosophy does not function this way.

25. See Johnston (2004) for attempts to avoid appealing to indiscriminability properties to explain how experiences can "match."

Chapter 7

Subject and Object in the Contents of Experience

W E BEGAN PART III WITH FOUR QUESTIONS ABOUT THE ROLE OF the objects we see in experience. So far, in response to Q1 and Q3, I've argued that phenomenal states are not individuated by the objects we see. This conclusion, however, played no role in the response to Q2, which is that experiences can have both objectually singular and objectually nonsingular contents. We can now turn to Q4: how does the phenomenal character of experiences that present public, external objects differ from the phenomenal character of those that do not?

Some visual experiences incorporate entoptic phenomena traditionally classified as visual sensations, such as the experience of "seeing stars" or of enjoying a red phosphene. On the face of it, the visual sensations differ systematically in their phenomenal character from visual perceptual experiences. In this chapter I will explore these phenomenal differences. Using the method of phenomenal contrast, I will argue that the phenomenal differences go along with representational differences and that these representational differences provide us with another case in which K-properties are represented in experience. The target hypothesis will be that visual perceptual experiences represent the objects we see both as independent of the subject and as perceptually connected to the subject, in senses that I will clarify. An analogous claim holds for hallucinations.

Both of these relations—subject-independence and perceptual connectedness—are prominent in the history of philosophy.

175

Numerous philosophers have held that the objects of perception in fact depend on the subject. Berkeley held that the objects of perception are ideas, which have to be constantly perceived in order to continue existing. Locke and later sense-datum theorists held that the direct objects of perception (such as sense-data) depend on being perceived, although the indirect objects of perception (such as ordinary objects) do not. Contemporary philosophers more often hold that the direct objects of perception are ordinary objects, which are independent of the subject's perception of them.

One can also ask if the objects of perception are *represented* as independent of the subject. This question is distinct from whether the objects of perception are subject-independent. Even if Berkeley and Locke are right that we perceive subject-dependent entities, these entities might be presented to us as subject-independent. Conversely, subject-independent objects that we perceive might not be presented to us as subject-independent. In the *Treatise*, Hume seems to suggest that subject-independence is never presented in perception:

> As to the independency of our perceptions on ourselves, this can never be an object of the senses; but any opinion we can form concerning it must be derived from experience and observation.[1]

I will be arguing that the stance Hume seems to take here is wrong. The objects we seem to see are presented to us as subject-independent.

Perceptual connections between subject and object have also attracted much attention from philosophers. In typical experiences of seeing external objects, the objects causally affect the visual system, and many philosophers have argued that such causal relations are partly constitutive of seeing itself.[2] John Searle

---

1. Hume 1978\1888, book 1, section 2, 191),
2. See, for instance, Grice's defense of this claim (1961).

(1983, chap. 3) has gone further, to argue that these causal relations are also represented in visual experience. As before, the two issues can be distinguished: many philosophers agree that causal relations connect us to what we see, but disagree with Searle's claim that such relations are presented as obtaining in our visual experiences.[3]

Another kind of perceptual connection involves the way that experiences depend on movement. In typical cases of seeing ordinary objects, unlike in cases of mere sensation, one can take different perspectives on the object perceived. In contrast, phosphenes cannot be viewed from different angles. One might say that S is *perspectivally connected* to an object when S's visual phenomenology depends on her perspectival relation to that object. (This notion will be refined later.) Once again, one could distinguish the claim that such perspectival connectedness is necessary for seeing[4] from the claim that, in experiences of seeing, objects are represented as perspectivally connected to the subject of the experience. I will argue that perspectival connectedness, like subject-independence, is indeed represented in visual perceptual experiences. There are in effect two kinds of objects of visual experience. The first, associated with visual perceptual experiences, look to stand in the perceptual relations that I will go on to describe. The second, associated with visual sensations, do not.

7.1 Subject-Independence and Perspectival Connectedness

Subject-Independence

There are various ways to make more precise the idea that the nature of a perceived object is independent of the subject. One notion of subject-independence focuses on the independence of

3. See the essays in Van Gulick and Lepore (1991, part 4).
4. Something close to this claim is defended by Noë (2003).

a thing's *existence* from the experience that the subject has in seeing it. An object is subject-independent in this sense if the course of its existence does not coincide with the course of the experience that the subject has in seeing it, or if it merely coincides accidentally. An entity that is subject-independent in this sense can persist beyond the course of the experience of a subject's seeing it.

A second notion of subject-independence focuses on the independence of a thing's *properties* from the experience that the subject has in seeing it. A perceived object is subject-independent with respect to some of its properties if its having those properties does not vary systematically with whether anyone is perceiving it, or with the specific perceptual experience they have. For example, a perceived object is subject-independent with respect to location properties when its location does not depend on the experience that the subject has in perceiving it. It is clear that the claim that an object is subject-independent with respect to location properties does not entail that it is subject-independent with respect to all properties, or with respect to its existence. But if an object's location properties are independent of the experiences a subject has in perceiving that object, this suffices for the object to be subject-independent in one important sense.

In what follows, I will focus on the second kind of subject-independence, and more specifically, on subject-independence with respect to location properties. An object o is subject-independent in this sense just in case the conditional (SI) is true:

(SI) If S changes her perspective on o, then o will not thereby move.

I'll say that a subject S *changes her perspective on o* just in case S substantially changes the position of her visual apparatus relative to o. Normally, the visual apparatus in question is the eyes, as opposed to prosthetic devices or instruments such as periscopes or telescopes. From now on, I'll talk only about eyes.

I will argue that visual perceptual experiences represent this sort of subject-independence.

Perspectival Connectedness

Typically, the objects we see look different to us depending on our perspective on the object. The notion of perspectival connectedness makes this idea more precise. A subject is perspectivally connected to an object o just in case the following conditional (PC) is true:

> (PC) If S substantially changes her perspective on o, her visual phenomenology will change as a result of this change.

The conditionals (SI) and (PC) are related in the following way. When (SI) is true for some perceiver and object perceived, there are also relations that one would expect to hold between that object, the perceiver's experiences, and movements of her eyes. Perspectival connectedness is one such relation.

The conditionals (SI) and (PC) correspond to certain of the subject's expectations. The expectations are qualified by background assumptions, as most expectations are. In the case of (PC), it is not assumed that the consequent will hold if the antecedent does, no matter what else happens. Rather, it is assumed by the subject that the consequent will hold if the antecedent does, *and* if her eyes start out and remain open and nothing suddenly occludes her new view of the object. In contrast, in the case of the English sentences used to state instances of (PC), it will at least vary with the context of use, whether or not such assumptions are part of the antecedent. So it is not part of the theses defended here that the contents of experiences that represent these conditionals will exactly mirror the contents of natural-language sentences containing the same words as the ones used to state (PC). An analogous point holds for (SI).

In many cases, the subjects of visual experience will have expectations with consequents that are more specific than those in (PC). For instance, if one is looking at a flowerpot, one does not simply expect that if one moves one's eyes relative to the flowerpot, one's visual phenomenology will change in some way or other. One expects it to change in specific ways. For instance, one typically expects specific other parts of the flowerpot to come into view, and one expects these unseen parts to be continuous in various respects with the seen parts and discontinuous in others. Alternatively, one might have acquired bizarre expectations about what one will see when one views the flowerpot from another angle; perhaps one expects that a silent miniature city has been built on its backside, which will be seen if one peers around the flowerpot. It is compatible with my claim that the relatively unspecific conditional (PC) is represented in experience that in addition, certain more specific conditionals are also represented. I will return to this issue later.

Do We Represent Subject-Independence and Perspectival Connectedness?

In the rest of this section, I will argue that we typically represent, in some part of our cognitive system, that the objects we see satisfy (SI) and (PC). It is a further question whether any of our visual experiences represent that this is so. That conclusion will be defended later.

Suppose I am looking at a telephone under ordinary circumstances. Normally, the following conditionals will be true, where x is the telephone:

- If I move my eyes, x will not thereby move.
- If I change my perspective on x, my visual phenomenology will change as a result of this change.

These conditionals are not both true for all things x that a subject can see. For instance, they are not always true when x is the sky or the parts of an enormous uniform expanse of which one is seeing only a relatively small portion. I will return later on to other cases of seeing objects in which the conditionals are false. For now, what's important is that in perceptions of ordinary objects such as fish and tables, these conditionals tend to be true with respect to the objects seen. They could in principle (in a world quite different from ours) be false, if moving one's eyes itself brought the things viewed with it, in the way that eyeglasses when worn (or other things connected to heads) move with head movement. But, as a matter of fact, our eyes are not connected in this way to the things that we see. When it comes to the things we see, the conditionals overwhelmingly tend to be true.

Now imagine looking at a telephone, then turning away from it to ask someone a question but continuing to have exactly the same sort of visual phenomenology as the experience with which you began, instead of seeing the person you initially turned to talk to. Or imagine peering around the back of the telephone to see where to plug in the cord and finding that your view of the telephone didn't change at all—that exactly the same parts of it were visible and your visual phenomenology had not changed at all. In other words, suppose you seemed to move your head in either of these ways but that your visual phenomenal state stayed exactly the same, so that you did not have the phenomenology of seeing the person you turned to talk to or of seeing different parts of the telephone. In this bizarre combination of experiences, you would feel that you had done something—namely, moved your head—which normally would change the perspective from which you see the telephone, and yet no new parts of the telephone had come into view. So deeply ingrained is the assumption that our eyes can move independently of the scene that we are seeing that, given this bizarre combination of experiences, you might well think that you had only imagined turning your head and that you hadn't managed to move it after all.

This suggests that not only are our eyes not attached to the things that we see, but, in addition, we seem to be sensitive to this fact. Another reason to think that we are sensitive to this fact is that we do not treat it as an open possibility that, in peering (or trying to peer) around the side of a telephone, the telephone will move with us, preventing us from getting the view that we want. If we did hold this possibility open, then we would take measures to make sure the phone stayed put as we moved to get a better view of it.

So, we don't normally take it to be an open possibility that the movements of the things we see systematically depend on the movements of our eyes. We assume that our eyes move independently of the things we see and that substantial head movements change one's visual phenomenology and bring other parts of things into view. It is clear, then, that our cognitive system represents the two conditionals above in some way. But it is not yet clear that they are represented in visual experiences.

7.2 COMPLEX CONTENTS

In John Searle's 1983 book *Intentionality* (chap. 3), he proposed that visual experiences have contents with the following form:

> (Searle) There is a red fish at L and the fact that there is a red fish at L is causing this experience.

Searle's contents focus on the causal dependence of the experience on the things seen. In contrast, the contents involving the conditionals (SI) and (PC) focus on the *in*dependence of the thing seen from experiences. In a case where you see something that looks like a red fish, the contents associated with these conditionals could have the following forms:

> There is an x such that if I change my perspective on x, then x will not thereby move, and x is a red fish at L.
> There is something perspectivally connected to this experience that is a red fish at L.

More generally, my proposal is that when S has an experience of object-seeing, the contents of the experience typically include contents of these forms:

> There is an x such that if I change my perspective on x, then x will not thereby move, and x is F.
> There is something perspectivally connected to this experience that is F.

When experiences have contents of these forms, I will say that they represent the conditionals (SI) and (PC). I've chosen nonsingular contents to illustrate, but singular contents could represent (SI) and (PC) as well.

Let's say that when an experience represents either a causal relation or a perceptual relation such as (SI) or (PC) between the subject, the subject's experience, or her perceptual apparatus, on the one hand, and something that the subject seems to see, on the other, the resulting contents are *complex*.[5] When experiences do not represent any such relation, we can call the resulting contents *simple*. So, one could argue against the view that experiences of object-seeing represent (SI) and (PC) by arguing that experiences have only simple contents.

Let a *simple view* be any view according to which visual perceptual experiences have only simple contents. And let's say that the *complex view* is the view that visual perceptual experiences represent (SI) and (PC).[6] To decide between the simple and the complex view, I'll employ the method of phenomenal contrast.

7.3 THE GOOD AND THE ODD

In this application of the method of phenomenal contrast, the target experience will be a typical case of seeing an ordinary object, and I'll call it the Good experience.[7] The contrasting experience

5. Another example of a complex relation would be the relation an experience stands in to an object when the experience is an experience of perceiving the object.

6. More exactly, the complex view says that the contents of visual perceptual experiences include contents of the form: There is an x such that if I change my perspective on x, x will not thereby move, and x is F; and there is something perspectivally connected to this experience that is F, where F is replaced with specific predicates.

7. The Good experience is a specific unrepeatable experience. In contrast, in the discussion of Naïve Realism in 2.5, "Good experiences" is a

will be odd, so I'll call it the Odd experience. The Good and the Odd will be as similar as possible, but it will be plain that the conditionals (SI) and (PC) are not represented in any way in the Odd experience. I think the Good experience and the Odd experience plainly differ phenomenally. The simple view has to either disrespect this verdict, find simple contents with respect to which the experiences differ, or else deny that there is any representational difference. I will argue that none of these options is satisfactory. The complex view, in contrast, can respect the verdict very easily.

The phenomenal contrast between the Good and the Odd emerges from the following case. Suppose you are looking at a tiny doll. You take yourself to be in the usual sort of circumstance with respect to the doll, so you take the conditionals (SI) and (PC) to be true with respect to her and to your experience. Moreover, you are correct: you are seeing a doll. You even play with the doll a bit, putting it into the little hands of its owner and then back on a shelf in front of you. Then your attention moves on to other things.

After an hour or so, however, something odd happens. You look back at the doll on the shelf and find that it seems to have lost its independence: it moves with movements of your head as if you were wearing a helmet with an imperceptible arm extending from the front, keeping the doll in your field of view. You hypothesize that someone has somehow attached the doll to your eyeglasses using a very thin string, without your knowing it.

So far, nothing in the story suggests that you would cease to take the conditionals (SI) and (PC) to hold with respect to the doll.

---

label for a class of non-hallucinatory experiences whose exact definition varies from one version of Naïve Realism to the next. So the same word is being used in different ways. As it happens, the Good experience will belong to the class of Good experiences, however defined, given that it is not a hallucination or illusion of any sort. But its status as non-hallucinatory is not essential to its contrast with the Odd experience. The Odd experience would be just as different phenomenally from a hallucinatory version of the Good experience.

But now suppose that the strange sequence of visual experiences continues in an even stranger vein. You decide to test the eyeglass hypothesis by moving your eyes without moving your head, and you find that the doll seems to move with your eyes as well. It seems to be sensitive to the slightest eye movement. And things get even stranger. When you close your eyes, you continue having a visual experience as of a doll. And when you try, with your eyes open, to put an opaque object right in front of the doll to block it from your view, your visual experience persists in being a visual experience as of a doll. Overall, your experience of the doll comes to operate much like the experience of "seeing stars" from being hit on the head or from standing up too quickly. Just as nothing can occlude the "stars," nothing can occlude the "doll"; and just as you can "see stars" while you are seeing other things, so it is that you continue to see things in the normal way even when the "doll" won't leave your field of view. As with "seeing stars," the apparent position of the "doll" is highly sensitive to eye movement.

If the visual experience as of a doll persisted despite such efforts at occlusion (by eyelids or by anything else), then the "dollesque" experience would lose its contingency on your movements. In response to such a series of bizarre experiences, one would reasonably come to regard the conditional (PC) as having a practically impossible antecedent. This seems tantamount to ceasing to represent it at all.[8] Compare the case of "seeing stars," when it is (or quickly becomes) obvious that you cannot change the position of your eyes relative to the "stars." There is little

8. Why couldn't conditionals with impossible antecedents be represented? There seems to be no bar to believing whatever they express. But the kind of representation that matters here is the kind that reflects our expectations about things. The conditional structure of (SI) and (PC) is just supposed to reflect that they are expectations. The claim about the bizarre sequence of experience is that it would remove the expectations reflected in the conditionals.

temptation to suppose that the conditionals are nonetheless taken to be true with respect to "stars" and the starry experiences.

Supposing that we have arrived at a case in which the conditionals cease to be represented in any way at all with respect to any dollesque experience, we can now describe the relevant pair of experiences. One is Good: that is, it is a paradigmatic case of seeing an external public object. And one is Odd: that is, the subject of the experience does not represent in any way at all in her cognitive system that the thing she seems to see is subject-independent or perspectivally connected to her experience. When the subject has the Odd experience, the subject does not in any way take the conditionals to be true—either at the level of belief, supposition, imagination, or visual experience.

The Good experience is the one had near the start of the series, when you put the doll on the shelf. The Odd experience is the one had at the end of the series, when the "doll" has (so to speak) been following you around, and you are standing in exactly the position you were in when you had the first experience, facing the same shelf where the doll was previously standing. So the two experiences being compared are momentary experiences. But the Odd experience, though momentary, occurs in an odd sequence of experiences (hence the name). What makes the sequence odd is that it violates some of your expectations—the ones expressed by the conditionals (SI) and (PC).

Having had the doll image follow your gaze around, could it nevertheless look to you as if there is a doll on the shelf, in just the way the doll itself looked to you when you saw it on the shelf earlier? If it could, then the phenomenal character of the visual parts of the Good and the Odd experiences is the same. If it couldn't, then the phenomenal character of the Good and the Odd differs.

The phenomenal contrast between the Good and the Odd can be brought into focus by considering a pattern of sensitivity and insensitivity. In the Odd experience, the apparent position of the doll is highly sensitive to the slightest movements of your eyes and insensitive to efforts at occlusion, either by eyelids or anything else. These sensitivities are not manifested at the very moment of the Odd experience, but the Odd experience happens just after they have been manifested. The same pattern is found in visual sensations, which are also sensitive to eye movements and impervious to attempts at occlusion.[9]

This pattern seems to be accompanied by a distinctive phenomenal character. If you look at a starry night sky and then (say, as the result of standing up too quickly) begin to "see stars," it would not look as if there were now more stars in the sky. One could make a similar point about fireflies in the air. Conversely, if you were "seeing stars," and looked up at the starry sky, one would not seem to "see" more "stars." The same holds for phosphenes. If you see a reddish shadow projected on a white wall and then begin to enjoy a vivid red phosphene, it need not look as if the wall has sprouted another reddish shadow. Conversely, if you start out enjoying a reddish phosphene and then see a reddish shadow on the wall, it need not feel as if you are enjoying two reddish phosphenes.[10] Similarly, in having an Odd experience

9. As the Odd experience is described in the doll case, there is an image of a doll that moves with the eye. One way this could happen is if the instability of the fixation point were eliminated by constraining the head and moving the visual scene to compensate for the usual small movements of the eye. However, such an image would not last very long since such retinal images are known to fade away after a few seconds. (See Tulunay-Keesey [1982].) The doll case, however, does not rely on predicting what would happen if the doll image did move with the eye in any empirical circumstance. What's crucial to the doll case is the claim that it is possible that there is a phenomenal difference between the Good case and a case in which one does not expect the conditionals to hold. The description of the odd sequence in which a doll seems to move with the eye is a means of making vivid one way in which one might come to lose those expectations.

10. Note that for there to be such phenomenal contrasts, it need not be the case that phosphenes or "stars" are *never* reasonably mistakable for shadows or real stars (or fireflies).

embedded in an experience of seeing a real doll on a shelf, it would not look as if there were two dolls on the shelf side by side, or as if there were suddenly two odd "dolls." Given these similarities, to explain away the appearance of a phenomenal contrast (e.g., by using the strategy described in 6.5), one would also have to explain away the appearance of all phenomenal contrasts between seeing stars and "seeing stars," and more generally between visual sensations and (pure) visual perceptual experiences.

One might grant that there is a phenomenal difference between the Good and the Odd experiences but at the same time deny that it is a difference in sensory phenomenology, analogously with the proposals involving non-sensory phenomenology discussed in part II. In the case of kinds, we argued that the target visual perceptual experiences need not be accompanied by occurrent, phenomenally conscious non-sensory states that represent K-properties. This point is even stronger for the class of visual perceptual experiences taken as a whole. There is no good candidate for a non-sensory phenomenally conscious state—whether occurrent or not—that accompanies every visual perceptual experience.

Alternatively, one might grant that there is a phenomenal difference between the Good and the Odd experiences but deny that there is any representational difference between them, just as with the raw-feel proposals discussed in connection with kind properties and causal properties in part II. According to this proposal, the doll in the Good experience and the "doll" in the Odd experience looks to have exactly the same properties. If this is correct, then in both experiences there looks to be a doll on the shelf that is a perfectly ordinary doll (at least, if this is how things look in the Good experience, then this option says it looks this way in the Odd experience). But once it has been granted that there is a difference as to which properties each "doll" seems to have, this position seems implausible.

If these two options are ruled out, then there is a phenomenal contrast between the Good and the Odd that illustrates a more general contrast between visual perceptual experiences and visual sensations, and that contrast, in turn, goes with a contrast between the contents of the Good and the Odd. The central question is then which sorts of contents are most adequate to the phenomenal contrast.

Accounting for the Phenomenal Contrast

Here is a hypothesis: the visual part of the Good experience has complex contents, whereas the visual part of the Odd experience has simple contents. From now on, I'll drop "visual part of" and just refer to these parts as Good and Odd, or the Good experience and the Odd experience.

An initial reason to believe this hypothesis is that the simple contents of the Good and the Odd experiences are plausibly the same. The "doll" in the Odd case does not seem to be behind you; it seems to be in front of you. As the case is described, in each experience the doll looks to have the same color, shape, and texture properties: the faces look the same, their hair looks the same, and so on. So it seems, at least prima facie, that resources besides simple contents will be needed to account for the difference in content.

A second reason to believe the hypothesis is that, in the doll case, it is losing one's expectations that the conditionals (SI) and (PC) hold that makes a phenomenal difference between the Good and the Odd experiences. One straightforward account of the phenomenal difference is that, in the move from the Good to the Odd experience, these very conditionals cease to be represented in visual experience.

A third reason to believe the hypothesis is suggested by the phenomenal similarity between the Odd experience and typical "visual sensations," on the one hand, and the phenomenal similarity between the Good experience and other visual perceptual experiences, on the other. A natural suggestion about how these classes of experience differ is that in visual perceptual experiences, objects are presented as being denizens of the external world rather than as mind-dependent entities of some sort. Phosphenes do not typically look to be denizens of the external world. Going along with this, if visual perceptual experiences were neutral as to whether the objects seen were mind-dependent or not, then it *would* look as if we could add the "stars" to the sky when "seeing stars," or that we could add a shadow to the wall while enjoying a phosphene. But it does not look this way.

I've offered some considerations favoring the view that the Good experience has complex contents, whereas the Odd experience has simple contents. In arguing against these considerations, the fan of the view that the Good experience has simple contents—the simple view introduced at the end of section 7.2—can try to give a more sophisticated account of the phenomenal contrast between the Good and the Odd experiences. I will now consider five versions of such an account and argue that none of them is adequate.

The first version says that the Odd experience does not represent anything at all, whereas the Good experience does, and does so by having simple contents. This version of the simple view makes the Odd experience either a "raw feel" or perhaps a sense-datum that is simply "given" to the subject, where in neither case is the subject in a state with accuracy conditions. This view seems wrong. In the Odd experience, the "doll" does not look to be behind the subject; instead, it looks to be in some other direction from the subject. So the property of being in such a direction is a property that, it seems, the experience represents the "doll" as having. If the "doll" is a sense-datum, then the experience is correct only if the sense-datum has the features that the experience attributes to it, or only if there is a public object that is appropriately related to the sense-datum and that has the properties that the "doll" looks to have.

The second version of the simple view is that, whereas the Good experience has simple contents, the Odd experience has the negative complex contents:

> There is an x such that if I move my eyes, x will thereby move, and
> x is not perspectivally connected to this experience, and x is F.[11]

In effect, this proposal says that, whereas the Good experience is neutral on whether the doll exists independently of the subject, the Odd experience is not so neutral. This position thus posits the following asymmetry: whereas expecting that the conditionals do not hold gives you non-neutral, negative experiential contents, expecting that the conditionals do hold—which, of course, is the normal expectation—leaves your experience neutral on whether they hold.

This asymmetry seems unmotivated to the extent that it relies on the idea that only abnormal expectations filter down to visual phenomenology. The extent to which any expectations affect perceptual experiences of any sort is admittedly controversial (as was noted in 6.7), though circumstantial evidence for it was offered in the discussion of kind properties in chapter 4.[12] But if there is any penetration of visual experience by other cognitive states at all, it is unlikely to be limited to abnormal expectations. There is nothing abnormal about the expectations concerning subject-independence and perspectival connectedness, yet gaining these expectations brings about a change in visual phenomenology and presumably, losing them would too.

The third version of the simple view is that the Odd experience represents the "doll" as being in a space discontinuous from physical space: this would be "mental space," home to apparently mind-dependent entities such as phosphenes. Note that this proposal is not committed to there being such a thing as mental space

---

11. Another sort of negative complex content would be: It is not the case that anything perspectivally connected to this experience is F. This seems to be a nonstarter, however, as it would count the Odd experience as veridical when there is no real doll on the shelf in front of the perceiver. The considerations raised in the text against the other negative complex content apply to this proposal as well.

12. On cognitive penetrability, see notes 5 and 7 from the introduction.

or to mental entities that dwell there; it is merely committed to the view that the Odd experience presents there being such a thing. (Although, if there are no such things, then the resulting contents are never true; hence, the experiences that have them are never veridical—and perhaps could never be, depending on whether it is merely contingent that there is no such thing as mental space harboring mental entities.) According to this proposal, the contents of both the Good experience and the Odd experience have the form:

There is a doll at L,

where the only admissible values for L in the Good experience are locations in physical space, and the only admissible values for L in the Odd experience are locations in mental space.

The third version relies on there being a difference between experientially representing something as being in mental space, on the one hand, and experientially representing something as being in physical space, on the other. What exactly would the Odd experience represent when it represents the odd "doll" as being located in mental space? Given that the point of the proposal is to account for the contrast between the Good experience and the Odd experience, the best specifications would seem to focus on what is most clearly phenomenally adequate to the Odd experience. One option is that x is represented as being in mental space just in case it is represented as being such that if the subject's eyes move, then x will move. Another option is that x is represented as being in mental space just in case it is represented as being something that the subject cannot view from different perspectives. But note that these two options amount to the same proposal as given in the second version of the simple view, which posited negative complex contents for the Odd experience and simple contents for the Good experience. These options thus do not add anything new to the dialectic.[13]

13. Still another option would be that x is represented as being in mental space exactly when it is represented as having only two dimensions. But appearing to have two dimensions does not seem to suffice for

The fourth version of the simple view proposes yet another way in which the representational difference between Good and Odd is a difference in spatial content. It posits simple contents for the Good experience and holds that the Odd experience is indeterminate with respect to whether the "doll" is at any of a range of locations in physical space or at some location in mental space. According to this version of the simple view, then, if there were a doll at the right location in physical space, the Odd experience would be correct.

Since this version of the simple view, like the third version, relies on a distinction between representing locations in physical space and representing locations in mental space, it, too, incurs the burden of specifying what this difference is. Here it will face exactly the same options since, once again, the most direct approach to phenomenal adequacy with respect to the Odd experience is that the contents are negative complex contents. And once again, this adds nothing new to the dialectic.

According to the fifth and last version of the simple view, the Good and the Odd experiences differ in their spatial content, where both contents are simple but the notion of mental space does not enter in. Both contents could be approximately expressed by the sentence, "There is something at location L with features F," where F are features that the doll in the Good experience looks to have, but the exact value of "L" in each case differs, according to this proposal. More specifically, the spatial contents of the Good experience specify a location on the shelf, and the spatial contents of the Odd experience are indeterminate over a range of locations in the space outside the body. One might try to draw support for this proposal from the fact that in some cases that are phenomenally similar to the Odd experience, such as some afterimages or

---

appearing to be in mental space, since that is not where scenes depicted on flat surfaces, with no representation of perspective, seem to be. Think of a drawing of a house that does not purport to represent it as extending forward or backward.

cases of "seeing stars," the experiences seem indeterminate with
respect to how far away from the subject the "stars" are or the
afterimage is.

If such indeterminacy with respect to distance from the subject
were the key representational difference between the Good and
the Odd experiences, then we should expect that *no* experience
with the sort of phenomenal character exemplified by the Good
experience is indeterminate with respect to where it represents an
object to be. But some such experiences clearly are indeterminate
in just this way. Consider two experiences of seeing a rabbit, in
both of which a rabbit looks to be in a certain direction and at least
distance D from the speaker. Let us suppose that there really is a
rabbit (that looks the way the experience characterizes it) in that
direction and at that distance but that, in one case, the rabbit is at
$L1$, whereas in the other, it is just slightly to the left, at $L2$. Now, if
the rabbit is far enough away, it seems plausible to suppose that
these experiences could be phenomenally indistinguishable from
one another. The question then arises whether either is falsidical
with respect to location. If we hold constant everything else about
the two situations besides the location of the rabbit seen, then it
seems implausible to classify one as falsidical with respect to location and the other as not. If both experiences are veridical, then
the experience will be indeterminate with respect to whether the
rabbit is at $L1$ or $L2$.

The upshot of the rabbit case is that it seems implausible to
suppose that the difference in whether (relatively) determinate or
indeterminate locations are attributed to the doll has much to do
with the sort of phenomenal difference there is between the Good
and the Odd experience. That is a reason to reject this last way of
pursuing the simple view.

Other Complex Views

I've considered and rejected five proposals for how the contents of the Good and the Odd might differ, consistent with the

contents of the Good experience being simple. Though I haven't shown that these proposals are the only ones there are, this makes a case for the view that the contents of experiences of visual perceptual experiences are not simple. I've also given several reasons to think that these experiences represent (SI) and (PC).

What, if anything, would be wrong with accepting these arguments against the simple view but holding that the Good experience has causal contents à la Searle, as opposed to representing (SI) and (PC)? This proposal would not be better than the simple view just canvassed. In fact, it is doubtful that Searle's causal contents account in any way for the phenomenal contrast between typical visual sensations and visual perceptual experiences. Some philosophers have doubted that there is any aspect of visual phenomenology that causal contents could reflect.[14] If they are correct, then the proposal that the Good experience has causal contents does not get off the ground. Searle himself suggests that if there is any aspect of visual phenomenology that the causal contents reflect, it is a difference between the phenomenal character of perceiving, in contrast to imagining.[15] The things one merely imagines do not seem to be "present" to one in the same way that the things one seems to see are present. Even if this is correct, however, it does not help with the phenomenal contrast at issue since phosphenes and "stars" and the odd "doll" *also* seem to be present, as opposed to merely imagined. So, if this is what is phenomenally distinctive about causal contents, then it cannot be causal contents that are had by the Good experience but are lacking in the Odd experience.

Where does that leave us? The hypothesis that the Good experience has simple contents does not seem to be workable.

14. These doubts are discussed in section 7.4.

15. As Searle notes, this consideration is perhaps most powerful for the case of tactile experience of pressure, such as feeling a knife in your back, but one might think a version of the same point holds for the distinction between visual experiences of seeing and visual imagery as well. See Searle's "Reply to Armstrong," in Van Gulick and Lepore (1991, 184).

A different hypothesis is that it has causal contents but does not represent (SI) and (PC). This hypothesis, however, does not seem to account for the contrast with the Odd experience. In contrast, the hypothesis that the Good experience represents (SI) and (PC) accounts for the phenomenal contrast with the Odd experience straightforwardly.[16] Doubtless there could be other versions of alternative views that have not been considered, but the considerations given so far go some way to defending the complex view.

I now want to return to a question raised in section 7.1 concerning whether conditionals such as (PC) but with more specific consequents are represented in visual experiences of object-seeing. Consider the proposal that the contents of a subject S's visual experience included a more specific version of (PC)—specific enough to reflect S's most specific expectations. Such a proposal would make the following prediction: that in the case where S's specific expectations are false—such as a case in which there is no miniature city on the backside of the flowerpot, as the subject bizarrely expects; or a case in which S expects the flowerpot to continue out of view in the normal way but it doesn't—the experience S has when she looks at the flowerpot will be falsidical, even if her experience does not reveal the expectations to be false. For example, suppose I have bizarre expectations about what sort of phenomenal character my visual experience will have if I peer around the other side of the flowerpot, but I don't actually peer around it. I just look at its facing surfaces, and so far as those surfaces are concerned, there is no falsidicality in my experience. If my specific expectations were included in the content of my

16. Why not think that just one of the conditionals (SI) or (PC) (or an existential generalization thereof) is represented in experience and not the other? One reason is that both expectations are lost in the Odd experience and both are in place in the Good experience. If either conditional is true, then typically the other will be true, and background expectations seem to be sensitive to this fact.

experience, then, since they are false, the proposal would classify my experience as falsidical. Is this classification intuitively correct?

It seems to me that intuitions about whether the experience is veridical or falsidical are not very strong either way. So, if there were an argument for the proposal that visual experiences represent a conditional along the lines of (PC) but with a more specific consequent, that argument would have to proceed in some way other than by appealing to such intuitions. One such strategy would be the method of phenomenal contrast. But this method relies on there being a stark phenomenal contrast between a case in which one sees the flowerpot and the specific expectations, and a case in which one sees the flowerpot and lacks those specific expectations but has slightly different ones. The intuition of phenomenal contrast here seems much weaker than the intuition in the doll case of a phenomenal contrast between the Good and the Odd experiences. If it is, then the strategy of appealing to phenomenal contrasts cannot get off the ground. So it seems best to consider it an open question whether a conditional such as (PC) but with a more specific consequent is represented in visual experiences of object-seeing until there is some third argumentative strategy that can settle the matter.

Is Every State of Seeing a Visual Perceptual Experience?

There are at least two kinds of states of seeing ordinary objects with respect to which it seems very implausible to suppose that they represent (SI) and (PC). First, in the original Odd experience, you are not really seeing an object, nor do you believe that you are—and, going with this, you don't expect to be able to interact with the "doll" in the ways you could interact with the (real) doll. But now consider a modified version of the Odd experience. It seems possible that you could really see a doll, while having the same negative expectations you have in the Odd case. And if that could happen, then in principle, it seems, the negative expectations could affect the experience in such a way as to give it the same phenomenology as in the Odd case. The result would be a case where one truly sees a doll, but sees it while having "odd" phenomenology. According to the argument I've given, this would be a case where the experience lacks complex content, even though it is a case of object-seeing.

Second, suppose you have a speck in your eye that you can see and that moves with the surface of your eyeball. To the extent that you deny the speck the status of being an object, this may be a borderline case of *object*-seeing, and it may even be a borderline case of seeing itself. But let us set these things aside. Suppose you grew accustomed to seeing the speck, and so ceased to expect (if you ever did) that you could interact with it in the ways described by the conditionals. This seems to be another case in which it is implausible to claim that it would look to you (or persist in looking to you) as if you could interact with the speck in those ways.

These two examples show that the verdict on the Good experience does not generalize to all cases of object-seeing. But this does not undermine the reason to think that that verdict on the Good case generalizes beyond that specific case. The Good experience is a completely typical experience. This makes it plausible to suppose that other equally typical experiences also represent these conditionals. In the next section, I will consider some other reasons to think that that verdict could not possibly be correct even for the single hypothetical Good case. Pending rejection of those, I conclude that there is strong reason to think that in a significant class of states of seeing objects, experiences represent the conditionals (SI) and (PC).

Most states of seeing ordinary objects—probably all but the exceptions just mentioned—are visual perceptual experiences. Hallucinatory visual perceptual experiences are not states of seeing but can have the same general kind of phenomenal character found in the typical cases of object-seeing on which we have focused. Even though, in hallucinations, there is no object that could figure in singular contents involving subject-independence and perspectival connectedness, hallucinatory visual perceptual experiences could still represent that these perceptual relations hold. So the reasons we've given for thinking that visual perceptual experiences that are cases of seeing represent (SI) and (PC) carry over to hallucinatory visual perceptual experiences as well.

Finally, although the doll case does not show that we represent that the objects seen *exist* independently of our experiences, it is not hard to imagine employing the method of phenomenal contrast to argue for the conclusion that experiences represent this kind of subject-independence as well. Such an argument would start with a pair of cases, where one is an ordinary case of object-seeing (e.g., a case of seeing a telephone) and the other is a case in which a telephone starts to exist only if I am seeing it and ceases to exist if I stop seeing it. If there is a phenomenal difference between these experiences, then one could try to argue that there must also be a representational difference in which the target experience represents the object as persisting independently of the experience of seeing it and the contrasting experience does not. If such an argument works, then combining this argument with the doll case would result in a two-part argument that visual perceptual experience can represent objects as being subject-independent with respect to both existence and location.

7.4 OBJECTIONS AND REPLIES

Now that the main argument has been given for the claim that visual perceptual experiences have complex contents involving the relations (SI) and (PC), let us consider some objections to the conclusion.

After Searle presented his view that experiences of seeing have causal contents, some philosophers objected that his view posited overly sophisticated phenomenology to creatures with visual experiences of seeing objects. Tyler Burge (1991, 204) wrote,

It seems implausible to me in the extreme to claim that we invariably visually experience causal relations between physical objects and our own perceptions.

Similarly, Matthew Soteriou (2000, 183) asks,

What aspect of the phenomenology of visual experience is left unexplained if one does not include the causal component in the content of visual experience? What discriminatory abilities are left unexplained if one does not include the causal component in the content of visual experience? Unless we have answers to these questions we will not have reason to accept Searle's account of the content of experience.

The main line of thought in these objections is that phenomenology does not support Searle's view. If the arguments surrounding the doll case work, then objections analogous to these have no force against the view defended here. The main support for the view is precisely that there is a dimension of the phenomenology of object-seeing that goes beyond the mere apparent presence of something that is common to both those visual experiences traditionally classified as visual sensations and to the more usual experiences of object-seeing. This dimension to the phenomenology of object-seeing is brought into focus by contrasting these two sorts of experiences, as the doll case allows us to do.[17]

There is a related objection, however, that cannot be answered by an appeal to phenomenology. Whereas the previous objection from Burge and Soteriou says that causal contents are not needed to account for the phenomenology of typical experiences of object-seeing, this objection says that such experiences cannot have causal contents because they are cognitively too sophisticated.

---

17. Smith (2002, chap. 5) contains a discussion of this contrast that is similar to the contrast defended here, though it does not explicitly distinguish between the thesis that the phenomenology of object-seeing involves representing the conditionals in experience and the thesis that it simply involves the conditionals holding. For further discussion, see Siegel (2006b, sec. 6).

Having an experience of object-seeing, the objection goes, just isn't ever as cognitively sophisticated an affair as Searle's view makes it out to be. An objection like this is raised by David Armstrong (1991, 154):

> Could it be the case . . . that the intentional object of the dog's perceptions should include, besides an external scene including the dog's *bodily* relation to that scene, the self-referential component that the perception itself, something in the dog's mind, should be caused by the external scene? It seems a bit much. What concern has your average dog with its own perceptions? Is it even aware of having them?

Burge (1991, 205) raises a more elaborate objection along the same lines:

> Experience is something that is available for use by a subject's central cognitive system . . . for purposes of judgment and intention. [F]or a subject's judgments to make reference to visual experiences, the subject himself, not merely a sub-system of the subject, must be capable of making discriminations between experiences and physical objects, and of using these discriminations in a wide range of judgments, judgments which presumably would involve reasoning about the discriminations. . . . [T]hese distinctions cannot be drawn by many higher animals, children[,] and adults of low intelligence that nonetheless have visual experience of physical objects.

Presumably, there are certain discriminations that one must be able to make if one experientially entertains a content with a self-referential component (expressed by "this experience"), and the concern is that the dog, though able to see ordinary objects, cannot make those discriminations. A worry along the same lines is that representing the conditionals (SI) and (PC) would require a greater degree of self-awareness than is needed to have experiences of object-seeing.

Contents involving these conditionals, however, are not so cognitively sophisticated. One worry behind the objection is that awareness of one's own experiences or eyes is overly cognitively sophisticated. But even dogs have egocentric representations of locations and can keep track of their position in space as they move. In order for there to be such representations, there has to be some way of representing the place where the perceiver is located—that is, the origin point of the axes along which the creature represents things as being located and along which the creature moves. There is already a theoretical purpose for which unsophisticated versions of self-awareness must be posited. So it is not an objection against any of the claims defended here that they involve such representations.[18]

Another point of focus in the objections is the putative representation in experience of the very experience being had. According to Burge in the passage above, cognitively unsophisticated creatures cannot distinguish between their experience and physical objects. But if subjects could not draw this distinction, then we'd expect that their experience would remain neutral on whether what they saw (or seemed to see) was or wasn't part of their body, as opposed to being part of the physical object. This seems quite implausible. Presumably, Burge has in mind more sophisticated versions of representations of one's own experience; but once again, there seems to be a theoretical need for less sophisticated ones, in any case. The independence of objects from experience may be less difficult to cognize than the causal dependence of experiences on objects seen.

Here is a final objection to the conclusion that experiences of object-seeing represent (SI) and (PC). Suppose the content of a visual experience of seeing a table is evaluated with respect to a world in which the perceiver's eyes are closed. According to the objection, if the experience represents (SI) and (PC), then when they are so evaluated, they will be incorrect. But—the objection

18. For further theorizing about the nature of primitive first-personal (or "first-creature") representations, see Peacocke (2003) and Bermudez (1998).

goes—this seems false. Intuitively, the objector says, if one evaluates the contents of experience with respect to a world where one's eyes are closed, they should be true. So the view that experiences of object-seeing represent (SI) and (PC) makes a false prediction: it wrongly predicts that an experience will be falsidical when evaluated with respect to this circumstance, when in fact the experience will be veridical.

In reply, the conditionals really are true when evaluated with respect to the situation in which one's eyes are closed, and so there is no conflict with the putative intuition that the objection invokes. Even in a situation where my eyes are closed, it remains true that if I move my eyes substantially relative to an object, it won't thereby move. One might think that it is false that if I move my eyes relative to x, my visual phenomenology will change as a result of a change in which parts of x are visible to me. This is the conditional (PC). But if the conditional (PC) has built into its antecedent that my eyes are open, then it is not false in the situation imagined. What is false is a *different* conditional, one whose antecedent is the same as the antecedent of "If I move my eyes relative to x *and my eyes are closed*, then there will be a change in which parts of x are visible to me." This conditional is not the one at issue. Rather, the conditional at issue is one that expresses the expectations discussed earlier. It is clearly part of these expectations that one's eyes are open.

The final objection has a second reply that brings us to a point about methodology. The central claim of the objection is that, given a standard experience of object-seeing, the contents of that experience—whatever they are—still come out true when evaluated with respect to a situation in which the perceiver's eyes are closed. It is important to note that the central claim differs from the plainly true claim that any slice of the external world that one sees will remain as it is, even if one's eyes are closed—barring strange causal chains involving eye-closings and ignoring relations such as causation and other kinds of perceptual connectedness between eyes and other external things. What the objector takes issue with is the claim that some experiences represent such complex relations, in addition to the simple features of the slice of the external world.

It strikes me as doubtful that we have any intuitions one way or another about whether the contents of an experience of object-seeing are true in the relevant situation. Whatever force the objection has seems to come from mistaking the plainly true claim that simple features of the external world are not affected by closing one's eyes with the dubious claim that the contents of the relevant sort of experience, whatever they are, are true when evaluated with respect to a situation in which one's eyes are closed. There are no such sophisticated intuitions for us to rely on in theorizing about what contents these experiences of object-seeing have. The intuitions we can rely on are unsophisticated ones about phenomenal contrasts. From there, what's needed are considerations of the sort discussed in connection with the doll case.

The fact that there are no strong intuitions about veridicality with respect to the world where eyes are closed does not show that there are never intuitions about veridicality. We put some such intuitions to work in chapter 2. In the simplest cases, if you consider whether an experience had in world w is accurate with respect to world w^*, it is often easy to find factors which, if they didn't hold in w^*, would make the experience inaccurate. It is as easy to find these factors as it is to generate scenarios in which a given experience would be an illusion. For instance, if you consider an experience of seeing a fishtank had in world w, where Raz the fish looks to be at location L, and consider its status when location L is empty in w, then we have a paradigmatic case of illusion. Nothing changes when we shift to a case where location L has Raz in it in w but is empty in world w^*: the intuition that the experience is falsidical with respect to world w^* is just as strong as the intuition that it is falsidical in w, as we originally described it (when w is empty). The case that experiences are assessable for accuracy does not depend on our having firm intuitions, for every world-experience pair, about whether the experience is veridical or not with respect to that world. Indeed, if we had such intuitions, the question of which properties experiences represent would be much less puzzling. We could just consult our intuitions about the relevant cases and, that way, figure out which contents experiences have. The fact that we have some such intuitions corroborates our arguments for the Content View. The fact that we don't have such intuitions for every possible world-experience pair indicates that we need a method that goes beyond an appeal to intuition, as the method of phenomenal contrast does, so that we can discover which contents experiences have.

Chapter 8

The Strong Content View Revisited

In PART III I'VE DEFENDED TWO GENERAL CONCLUSIONS ABOUT THE contents of visual experience. First, all visual perceptual experiences have nonsingular contents. Second, they all represent (SI) and (PC). In visual perceptual experiences that incorporate visual sensations, objects of experience such as "stars" (when you "see stars") do not appear to stand in these perceptual relations to you, but they look to have other properties, such as location in a strange space, brightness, and motion. In addition to these two conclusions, I argued that phenomenal states are not individuated by any objects seen. A subject could be in the same (repeatable) phenomenal state, whether she was seeing Franco or hallucinating, and whether she was seeing Franco or Franco's twin.

We are now in a good position to examine the relationship between these conclusions and the Strong Content View introduced in 2.6. There we distinguished the Content View from the Strong Content View. According to the Strong Content View, all visual perceptual experiences consist fundamentally in the subject's bearing a propositional attitude toward the contents of her experience.

Our conclusions from part III do not entail the Strong Content View. But it would be natural to ask: Are there grounds for elevating these conclusions into a thesis about the nature of visual phenomenal states in general, according to which they consist entirely in the subject's bearing the same propositional attitude toward nonsingular contents? Here is one such thesis:

Internalist Strong Content View: All visual phenomenal states consist fundamentally in the subject's bearing the same propositional attitude toward nonsingular contents of her experience.

The Internalist Strong Content View (or Internalist SCV) is a thesis about visual phenomenal states in general. It is close to the traditional outlook discussed in the introduction, with which the Content View is commonly associated.[1] According to the traditional outlook, visual experiences form a single kind of mental state encompassing hallucinations along with perceptions, and phenomenally identical experiences have exactly the same contents. The Internalist SCV allows that experiences besides phenomenal states, such as states of seeing, can be experiences and can have singular contents. But the Internalist SCV is a substantive thesis about the nature of visual phenomenal states. It is at odds with Naïve Realism and with the idea that some visual phenomenal features are raw feels.

If someone antecedently favored the Internalist SCV, they might feel encouraged by the conclusions we have drawn so far. If the Internalist SCV is true, then it must be possible to incorporate paradigmatic visual sensations that figure in visual perceptual experiences, such as phosphenes and "stars," into the propositional attitude—but we've discussed how that might be a difference at the level of contents. In addition, if the Internalist SCV is true, there has to be a propositional attitude that can play the role it describes. It is not hard to identify constraints on such an attitude. They would presumably include these:

(a) the propositions are true with respect to a world just in case the experience is weakly veridical relative to that world;

(b) the propositions reflect the commitments of the experience;

---

1. The Internalist SCV is not the only way to make the Strong Content View internalist. It could also be made internalist without non-singular contents, for instance by invoking sense-data to which properties are attributed, or singular Meinongian contents.

(c) the propositions reflect the phenomenal character of the experience;

(d) the resulting state is not the kind of state that can or should be adjusted in response to evidence; and

(e) the propositions are conveyed to the subject.

These constraints reflect some of the differences between visual perceptual experience and belief.[2] While (a) is also a constraint on belief contents, arguably none of the others are. Constraint (d) does not apply to beliefs, since beliefs are sensitive to evidence: we can and should adjust what we believe according to the evidence that bears on those beliefs. In contrast, even when experiences may be influenced by non-perceptual states, such as moods, hypotheses, or desires, there does not seem to be such a thing as adjusting your experience in response to evidence, nor is there any associated norm governing experiences. Constraint (c) also does not apply to beliefs that are standing dispositional states, since these (in contrast to occurrent states) will not have any associated phenomenal character. To the extent that experiences are committal in a different way than beliefs are, (b) is also not a constraint on beliefs.

But to defend the Internalist SCV fully, other hurdles would need to be crossed. For one thing, given that it is about all visual phenomenal states, it applies even to experiences such as brain gray and the pink glow that you have when your eyes are closed. And it is far from obvious that there is any way that anything is presented as being in such experiences. If any visual experience is a Reidian sensation (raw feel), the simple kind you have with your eyes closed would probably be it. Furthermore, independently of any difficulties that pure visual sensations pose for the Internalist SCV, there must be some reason to think that all phenomenal

2. Arguably, they reflect a difference between sensory experience in general, and belief. The Internalist SCV could involve either a propositional attitude for sensory experience generally (compare Tye [2003] and Bourget [2010]), or a propositional attitude distinctive of visual experience.

aspects of visual experience—not just the paradigmatic visual sensations—have a place in the propositional attitude structure. The considerations raised against Reidian sensations in 4.2 and 5.5 give us reason to take the Internalist SCV seriously. But perception is a complex phenomenon, and none of the doubts cast on Reidian sensations along the way suffice to show that all phenomenal features of experience are representational features, or even that all phenomenal features of visual perceptual experiences supervene on their representational features. Some well-known putative counterexamples to this claim include blurred vision;[3] constancy phenomena involving color, shape, or size;[4] attentional shifts;[5] and other challenges may yet emerge. These phenomena cannot be treated in one fell swoop. To address them on their own terms, one would have to fill in the picture of the contents of experience further than we've done here, to show how Fregean modes of presentation, Russellian contents, or some other kind of accuracy condition answers these challenges. So while the Internalist SCV may ultimately be defensible, someone antecedently disposed to favor it shouldn't be too confident in its truth on the basis of the conclusions defended here unless they can give a detailed theory of the contents of experience that respects the complexity of these phenomena.

3. Boghossian and Velleman (1989), Smith (2008), Pace (2007), and Speaks, J. 2010. "Attention and Intentionalism." *Philosophical Quarterly* 60:239, 325–342.
4. Peacocke (1983), Block (1997), and Hellie (2006).
5. Nickel (2006) and Wu (2011).

References

Armstrong, D. 1991. "Intentionality, Perception, and Causality." In *John Searle and His Critics*, ed. R. van Gulick and E. Lepore, 149–58. Cambridge, MA: Blackwell.

Bach, K. 2007/1997. "Searle Against the World : How Can Experiences Find Their Objects?" In Savas L. Tsohatzidis (ed.), *John Searle's Philosophy of Language: Force, Meaning, and Mind*. Cambridge University Press.

Barrett, L., and M. Bar. 2009. "See It with Feeling: Affective Predictions during Object Perception." Theme issue, *Predictions in the Brain: Using Our Past to Generate a Future*, ed. M. Bar. *Philosophical Transactions of the Royal Society* B, 364:1325–34.

Barrick, C., Taylor, D. and Correa, E. 2002. "Color Sensitivity and Mood Disorders: Biology or Metaphor?" *Journal of Affective Disorders* 68:1,67–71.

Bayne, T., and D. Chalmers. 2003. "What Is the Unity of Consciousness?" In *The Unity of Consciousness: Binding, Integration, Dissociation*, ed. A. Cleeremans. New York: Oxford University Press, 23–58.

Bayne, T. 2009. "Perception and the Reach of Phenomenal Content." *Philosophical Quarterly* 59 (236): 385–404.

Bennett, A., and R. Rabbetts. 2004. *Clinical Visual Optics*. Edinburgh: Butterworth-Heineman.

Bermudez, J. L. 1998. *The Paradox of Self-Consciousness*. Cambridge, MA: MIT Press.

Block, N. 1990. "Inverted Earth." *Philosophical Perspectives* 4:53–79.

———. 1996. "Mental Paint and Mental Latex." *Philosophical Issues* 7:19–49.

———. 2002. "Concepts of Consciousness." In *Philosophy of Mind*, ed D. Chalmers, New York: Oxford University Press.

———. 2007. "Consciousness, Accessibility, and the Mesh between Philosophy and Neuroscience." *Brain and Behavioral* Science 30, 481–548

Boghossian, P., and J. D. Velleman. 1989. "Color as a Secondary Quality. *Mind* 98 (January): 81–103.

Boring, E. 1929. *A History of Experimental Psychology*. New York: Century.

Bourget, D. 2010. "Consciousness is Underived Intentionality" *Noûs* 44 (1): 32–58.

Brewer, B. 2006. "Perception and Content." *European Journal of Philosophy* 14 (2): 165–81.

Broackes, J. 2010. What Do the Color-Blind See? In *Color Ontology and Color Science*, ed. J. Cohen and M. Matthen. Cambridge, MA: MIT Press, 291–405.

Burge, T. 1991. "Vision and Intentional Content." In *John Searle and His Critics*, ed. R. van Gulick and E. Lepore, 195–213. Cambridge, MA: Blackwell.

Byrne, A. 2009. "Experience and Content." *Philosophical Quarterly* 59: 429–51.

Byrne, A., and Hilbert, D. 1997. *Readings on Color*. Vol. 1. Cambridge: MIT Press.

Byrne, A., and Logue, H. 2008. "Either/Or: Disjunctivism for Dummies." In *Disjunctivism: Perception, Knowledge, Action*, ed. F. Macpherson and A. Haddock, 57–94. Oxford: Oxford University Press.

Campbell, J. 2002. *Reference and Consciousness*. Oxford: Oxford University Press.

Chalmers, D. 2004. "The Representational Character of Experience." In *The Future for Philosophy*, ed. B. Leiter, 153–81. New York: Oxford University Press.

———. 2006. "Perception and the Fall from Eden" in *Perceptual Experience*, ed. T. Gendler and J. Hawthorne, 49–125. Oxford: Oxford University Press.

Chisholm, R. 1957. *Perceiving*. Ithaca, NY: Cornell University Press.

Churchland, P. 1988. "Perceptual Plasticity and Theoretical Neutrality: A Reply to Jerry Fodor," *Philosophy of Science* 55:167–87.

Clarke, A. 2000. *A Theory of Sentience*. New York: Oxford University Press.

———. 2004. "Sensing, Objects and Awareness: Reply to Commentators." *Philosophical Psychology* 17 (4): 553–79.

Dainton, B. 2000. *Stream of Consciousness*. New York: Routledge.

Davies, M., and Coltheart, M. 2000. "Pathologies of Belief," *Mind and Language* 15 (1): 1–46.

Dickie, I. 2011. "Visual Attention Fixes Demonstrative Reference by Elim-
inating Referential Luck". in *Attention: Philosophical and Psychological
Essays*. Eds. C. Mole, D. Smithies and W. Wu. New York: Oxford.

Dretske, F. 1999. "The Mind's Awareness of Itself." *Philosophical Studies*
95:103–24.

Dummett, M. 1981. *Frege: Philosophy of Language*. Cambridge, MA:
Harvard University Press.

Eberhardt, J. et al. 2004. Seeing Black: Race, Crime and Visual Processing." *Journal of Personality and Social Psychology* 87 (6): 876–93.

Egan, A. 2006. "Appearance Properties?" *Nous* 40 (3): 495–521.

———. 2010. "Projectivism without Error." In *Perceiving the World*, ed.
B. Nanay. New York: Oxford University Press.

Evans, G. 1982. *The Varieties of Reference*. Oxford: Oxford University
Press.

Farkas, K. 2006. "Indiscriminability and the Sameness of Appearance."
Proceedings of the Aristotelian Society 106., Part II, 205-25.

Fish, W. 2008. "Disjunctivism, Indistinguishability and the Nature of Hal-
lucination." In *Disjunctivism: Perception, Action and Knowledge*, ed.
F. Macpherson and A. Haddock, 144–67. Oxford: Oxford University
Press.

———. 2009. *Perception, Hallucination and Illusion*. Oxford: Oxford University Press.

Fleming, N. 1957. "Recognizing and Seeing As." *Philosophical Review* 66
(2): 161–79.

Fodor 1984. "Observation Reconsidered." *Philosophy of Science* 51:23–43.

———. 1988. "A Reply to Churchland's 'Perceptual plasticity and theoretical neutrality.'" *Philosophy of Science* 55:188–98.

———. 1997. "Special Sciences: Still Autonomous after All These Years."
Philosophical Perspectives 11:149–63.

———. 2006. *Hume Variations*. Oxford: Oxford University Press.

Foster, J. 2000. *The Nature of Perception*. Oxford: Oxford University Press.

Gibson, E. J., and R. D. Walk. 1960. "The 'visual cliff.'" *Scientific American*
202:67–71.

Ginet, C., 1975. *Knowledge, Perception and Memory*. Boston: D. Reidel.

Gopnik, A., C. Glymour, D. M. Sobel, L. E. Schultz, T. Kushnir, and
D. Danks. 2004. "A Theory of Causal Learning in Children: Causal
Maps and Bayes Nets." *Psychological Review* 111 (1): 3–32.

Grice, H. P. 1989. "The Causal Theory of Perception." In *Studies in the Ways of Words.* Cambridge, MA: Harvard University Press. (Orig. pub. 1961.)

Hansen, T., K, Gegenfurtner, M. Olkkonen, and S. Walter. 2006. "Memory Modulates Color Experience." *Nature Neuroscience* 9 (11), 1367–68.

Hawthorne, J., and K. Kovakovich. 2006. "Disjunctivism." *Proceedings of the Aristotelian Society* Supplementary Volume 80 (1) 145–83.

Heck. R. 2007. "Are There Different Kinds of Content?" In *Contemporary Debates in the Philosophy of Mind,* ed. J. Cohen and B. McLaughlin, 117–38. Oxford, UK: Blackwell.

Hellie, B. 2006. "Beyond Phenomenal Naivete." *Philosophers' Imprint* 6 (2): 1–24.

———. 2010. "An Externalist's Guide to Inner Experience." In *Perceiving the World,* ed. B. Nanay. New York: Oxford University Press.

———. n.d. "The Multidisjunctive Conception of Hallucination." In *Hallucination,* ed. F. Macpherson,. Cambridge, MA: MIT Press. Forthcoming.

———. ms. *Conscious Life. http://individual.utoronto.ca/benj/*

Hinton, J. 1973. *Experiences.* Oxford, UK: Clarendon.

Horgan, T. and Tienson, M. 2002. "The Intentionality of Phenomenology and the Phenomenology of Intentionality." In *Philosophy of Mind: Classical and Contemporary Readings,* ed. D. Chalmers, 520–33. New York: Oxford University Press.

Hume, D. 1978. *A Treatise of Human Nature,* ed. P. H. Nidditch. 2nd ed. Oxford, UK: Clarendon. (Orig. pub. 1888.)

Husserl, E. 1980. *On the Phenomenology of the Consciousness of Internal Time,* trans. J. B. Brough. Dordrecht, Netherlands: Kluwer. (Orig. pub. 1893.)

Hyslop, A. 1983. "On 'Seeing-As.'" *Philosophy and Phenomenological Research* 43 (4): 533–40.

Jackson, F. 1977. *Perception.* Cambridge: Cambridge University Press.

James, W. 1884. "What Is an Emotion?" *Mind* 9:188–204.

Johnston, M. 2004. "The Obscure Object of Hallucination." *Philosophical Studies* 120:113–83.

———. 2006. "Better Than Mere Knowledge." In *Perceptual Experience,* ed. T. Gendler and J. Hawthorne, 260–90. Oxford: Oxford University Press.

Kennedy, M, 2009. "Heirs of Nothing: Implications of Transparency." *Philosophy and Phenomenological Research*.79:3, 574–604.

Kind, A. 2007. "Restrictions on Representationalism." *Philosophical Studies* 134:405–27.

Koksvik, Ole, ms. *Intuition, Belief and Disposition to Believe. http://philrsss. anu.edu.au/~ole/*

Kriegel, U. 2007. "Intentional Inexistence and Phenomenal Intentionality." *Philosophical Perspectives* 21:307–40.

Kveraga, K. J., M. Bar, and J. Boshyan. 2009. "The Proactive Brain: Using Memory-based Predictions in Visual Recognition." In *Object Categorization: Computer and Human Vision Perspectives*, ed. S. Dickinson, M. Tarr, A. Leonardis, and B. Schiele. New York: Cambridge University Press.

Langsam, H. 2011 *The Wonder of Consciousness*. Cambridge, MA: MIT Press. Forthcoming.

Leibniz, G. W. 1996. *New Essay on Human Understanding*. Trans. and ed. P. Remnant and J. Bennett. New York: Cambridge University Press. (Orig. pub. 1705.)

Lepore, E., and R. van Gulick. 1991. *John Searle and His Critics*. Oxford: Blackwell.

Levin, D. T., and M. R. Banaji. 2006. "Distortions in the Perceived Lightness of Faces: The Role of Race Categories." *Journal of Experimental Psychology: General* 135:501–12.

Levine, J. 2003. "Experience and Representation." In *Consciousness: New Philosophical Perspectives*, ed. Q. Smith and A. Jokic. Oxford: Oxford University Press.

Lewis, D. 1980. "Veridical Hallucination and Prosthetic Vision." *Australasian Journal of Philosophy* 58 (September): 239–49.

Locke, J. 1975. *An Essay on Human Understanding*. Ed. P. Nidditch. Oxford, UK: Clarendon. (Orig. pub. 1698.)

Logue, H. 2011. "Good News for the Disjunctivist about One of the Bad Cases," *Philosophy and Phenomenological Research,* forthcoming.

Macpherson, F. 2012. "Cognitive Penetration of Colour Experience: Rethinking the Issue in Light of an Indirect Mechanism." *Philosophy and Phenomenological Research* 84/1, 24–62.

Martin, C. B. 1980. "Substance Substantiated." *Australasian Journal of Philosophy* 58:3–10.

Martin, M. G. F. 2002. "The Transparency of Experience." *Mind and Language* 17 (4): 376–425.

———. 2004. "The Limits of Self-Awareness." *Philosophical Studies* 120:37–89.

———. 2006. On Being Alienated. In *Perceptual Experience*, ed. T. Gendler and J. Hawthorne, 354–410. Oxford: Oxford University Press.

McDowell, J. 1996. *Mind and World*. Cambridge, MA: Harvard University Press.

McGinn, C. 1989 *Mental Content*. Oxford, UK: Blackwell.

———. 1996. "Another Look at Color." *Journal of Philosophy* 93 (11): 540.

McLaughlin, B. "Lewis on What Distinguishes Perception from Hallucination." In *Problems in Perception*, ed. K. Akins, 198–231. Oxford: Oxford Univers ity Press, 1996.

Michotte, A. 1963. *The Perception of Causality*. New York: Basic Books. (Orig. pub. 1946.)

Nichols, R. 2007. *Reid's Theory of Perception*. New York: Oxford University Press.

Nickel, B. 2007. "Against Intentionalism." *Philosophical Studies* 136 (3): 279–304.

Nida-Rumelin, M. 1996. "Pseudonormal Vision: An Actual Case of Qualia Inversion?" *Philosophical Studies* 82 (2): 145–57.

Noë, A. 2003. "Causation and Perception: The Puzzle Unravelled." *Analysis* 63:93–99.

Pace, M. 2007. "Blurred Vision and the Transparency of Experience." *Pacific Philosophical Quarterly* 88 (3): 328–54.

Pautz, A. 2009. "What Are the Contents of Experience?" *Philosophical Quarterly* 59:483–507.

———. 2010. "Why Explain Visual Experience in Terms of Content?" In *Perceiving the World*, ed B. Nanay, New York: Oxford University Press.

Payne, K. 2001. "Prejudice and Perception: The Role of Automatic and Controlled Processes in Misperceiving a Weapon." *Journal of Personality and Social Psychology* 81:1–12.

Peacocke, C. 1983. *Sense and Content*. Oxford: Oxford University Press.

———. 1992. *A Study of Concepts*. Cambridge, MA: MIT Press.

———. 2003. "Non-Conceptual Content: Kinds, Rationales, Relations." In *Essays on Non-Conceptual Content*, ed. Y. Gunther, 309–22. Cambridge, MA: MIT Press.

Perry, J. 1993. "The Problem of the Essential Indexical." Reprinted in *The Problem of the Essential Indexical and Other Essays*. New York: Oxford University Press.

———. 1993. "A Problem about Continued Belief." Reprinted in *The Problem of the Essential Indexical and Other Essays*. New York: Oxford University Press.

Pitt, D. 2004. "The Phenomenology of Cognition, or What Is It Like to Think That p?" *Philosophy and Phenomenological Research* 69 (1): 1–36.

Pylyshyn, Z. 1999. "Is Vision Continuous with Cognition? The Case for Cognitive Impenetrability of Visual Perception." *Behavioral and Brain Sciences* 22 (3): 341–65.

Raftopoulos, A. 2009. *Cognition and Perception*. Cambridge, MA: MIT Press.

Reid, T. 1997. *An Inquiry into the Human Mind: On the Principles of Common Sense*. University Park, PA: Pennsylvania State University Press. (Orig. pub. 1774.)

Rey, G. 1998. "A Narrow Representationalist Account of Qualitative Experience." *Philosophical Perspectives* 12:435–58.

Robinson, H. 1994. *Perception*. New York: Routledge.

Rubens, A. B., and D. F. Benson. 1971. "Associative Visual Agnosia." *Archives of Neurology* 24:305–16.

Russell, B. 1997. *The Problems of Philosophy*. New York: Oxford University Press. (Orig. pub. 1912.)

Saxe, R., and S. Carey. 2006. "The Perception of Causality in Infancy." *Acta Psychologica* 123 (September–October).

Schellenberg, S. 2011, "Ontological Minimalism about Phenomenology" *Philosophy and Phenomenological Research* 83/1, 1–40.

Scholl, B. 2002. *Objects and Attention*. Cambridge, MA: MIT Press.

Schwitzgebel, E. 2007. "Do We Have Tactile Experience of the Feet in our Shoes?" *Journal of Consciousness Studies* 14 (3): 58–76.

Searle, J. 1983. *Intentionality*. Cambridge: Cambridge University Press.

———. 1991. "Reply to Armstrong." In *John Searle and His Critics*, ed. E. Lepore and R. van Gulick. Oxford: Blackwell.

Shoemaker, S. 1996. "Unity of Consciousness and Consciousness of Unity." In *The First-Person Perspective and Other Essays*. Cambridge: Cambridge University Press.

———. 1994. "Phenomenal Character." *Nous* 28:21–38.

———. 2006. "On the Ways Things Appear." In *Perceptual Experience*, ed. T. Gendler and J. Hawthorne, 49–125. Oxford: Oxford University Press.

Sider, T. 2006. "Bare Particulars." *Philosophical Perspectives* 20:387–97.

Siegel, S. 2002. "The Role of Perception in Demonstrative Reference." *Philosophers' Imprint* 2 (1).

———. 2002. "Review of Austen Clarke, *Sensory Qualities*." *Philosophical Review* 111 (1): 135–38.

———. 2004. "Indiscriminability and the Phenomenal." *Philosophical Studies* 120:91–112.

———. 2005. "The Phenomenology of Efficacy." *Philosophical Topics* 33 (1): 265–84.

———. 2006a. "Subject and Object in the Content of Visual Experience." *Philosophical Review* 115 (3): 355–88.

———. 2006b. "Direct Realism and Perceptual Consciousness." *Philosophy and Phenomenological Research* 73 (2): 378–410.

———. 2008. "The Epistemic Conception of Hallucination." In *Disjunctivism: Perception, Action and Knowledge*, ed. by F. Macpherson and A. Haddock (Oxford: Oxford University Press), 205–24.

———. 2010. "Disjunctivism and Illusion." *Philosophy and Phenomenological Research* 80 (2): 384–410.

———. 2011. "Cognitive Penetrability and Perceptual Justification." *Nous/* forthcoming.

Siewert, C. 1998. *The Significance of Consciousness*. Princeton: Princeton University Press.

———. 2011. "Phenomenal Thought." In *Cognitive Phenomenology*, ed. Tim Bayne and Michelle Montague, Oxford, UK: Oxford University Press.

Smith, A. D. 2002. *The Problem of Perception*. Cambridge, MA: Harvard University Press.

———. n.d. "Disjunctivism and Illusion." *Philosophy and Phenomenological Research*. Forthcoming.

Soteriou, M. 2000. "The Particularity of Visual Perception." *European Journal of Philosophy* 8 (2): 173–89.

———. 2009. "The Disjunctive Theory of Perception." *Stanford Encyclopedia of Philosophy* (Fall).

Speaks. J. 2009. "Transparency, Intentionalism, and the Nature of Perceptual Content." *Philosophy and Phenomenological Research* 79 (3): 539–73.

———. 2010. "Attention and Intentionalism." *Philosophical Quarterly* 60:239, 325–342.

Strawson, G. 1994. *Mental Reality*. Cambridge, MA: MIT Press.

Stalnaker, R. 2003. "What Might Non-Conceptual Content Be?" In *Essays on Non-Conceptual Content*, ed. Y. Gunther. Cambridge, MA: MIT Press.

Stokes, D. (forthcoming) "Seeing and Desiring: A New Look at the Cognitive Penetrability of Experience," *Philosophical Studies*.

Sturgeon, S. 2008. "Disjunctivism about Visual Experience." In *Disjunctivism: Perception, Action and Knowledge*, ed. F. Macpherson and A. Haddock, 112–43. Oxford: Oxford University Press.

———. 2006. "Reflective Disjunctivism." *Proceedings of the Aristotelian Society* 80 (1): 185–216.

Thompson, B. 2006. "Colour Constancy and Russellian Representationalism." *Australasian Journal of Philosophy* 84:75–94.

———. 2009. "Senses for Senses." *Australasian Journal of Philosophy* 87 (1): 99–117.

———. 2010. "The Spatial Content of Experience." *Philosophy and Phenomenological Research* 81.

Travis, C. 2004. "The Silence of the Senses." *Mind* 113:57–94.

———. unpublished. "Comments on Siegel."

Tulunay-Keesey, U. 1982. "Fading of Stabilized Retinal Images." *Journal of Optical Society of America* 72:440–47.

Tye, M. 1995. *Ten Problems of Consciousness*. Cambridge, MA: MIT Press.

——— 2003. *Consciousness and Persons*. Cambridge, MA: MIT Press.

———. 2007 "Intentionalism and the Argument from No Common Content." *Philosophical Perspectives* 21 (1): 589–613.

Williamson, T. 1990. *Identity and Discrimination*. Oxford, UK: Blackwell.

Wright, W. 2003. "Projectivist Representationalism and Color." *Philosophical Psychology* 16:515–33.

Wu, W. n.d. What Is Conscious Attention? *Philosophy and Phenomenological Research*. Forthcoming.

Index

modes of presentation 57, 78, 151,
    210
moods 107

N

Naïve Realism 29, 39, 68, 72–76,
    135n.12, 183n.7
    Radical 65–66

O

object categorization 112,
    160–161n.12
occurrent thoughts 93n.7

P

Papineau, D. 78
Peacocke, C. 28n.2, 88, 100n.1,
    202n.18
perceptual constancies 89,
    178–181
    perspectival connectedness
        179–180
    subject-independence
        177–178
phenomenally conscious states
    20
phenomenal states 20, 23
phosphenes 24, 187
presentation 46–51, 156
Property View 71–72
propositions 77
Pure Object View 65

R

raw feels 56, 64, 94, 109–110, 124,
    139

recognition 100 (*see* object-
    categorization)
recognitional disposition, 100
Reid, T. 21, 72n.84
retention 127–128
Rich Content View 7
Russell. B. 71, 72n.47, 151, 153

S

science of consciousness 11–13
Searle, J. 176–177, 182, 195, 199, 201
seeing 20–23, 153–156
seeing-as 21
singular contents 15, 142
    objectual vs. predicative
        158–160
Siewert, C. 92n.14, 93n.16, 106
skepticism 7–8
Soteriou, M. 173n.23, 200
spectral inversion 89, 134
Stalnaker 78, 84, 86
Strong Content View (*see* contents)
Stümpf 33
subject-independence (*see*
    perceptual constancies)

T

Thesis K 7n.4
Thompson, B. 28n.2, 56–57,
    58n.28
tropes 58n.29
Travis 5n.2, 29, 60–65
truth 31n.4
two-dimensional theories of
    content (*see* contents)
Tye, M. 74n.50, 78, 84, 86,
    209n.2

CPSIA information can be obtained at www.ICGtesting.com
Printed in the USA
BVOW081919031012

302040BV00001B/116/P